Hand-Stitched Oasis

EMBROIDER REALISTIC ELEMENTS

Step-by-Step Guide with 35 Techniques

THERESA M. LAWSON

stashBOOKS®

an imprint of C&T Publishing

Text and photography copyright © 2024 by Theresa Marie Lawson

Photography and artwork copyright © 2024 by C&T Publishing, Inc.

PUBLISHER: Amy Barrett-Daffin

CREATIVE DIRECTOR: Gailen Runge

SENIOR EDITOR: Roxane Cerda

ASSOCIATE EDITOR: Karly Wallace

TECHNICAL EDITOR: Debbie Rodgers

COVER/BOOK DESIGNER: April Mostek

PRODUCTION COORDINATOR: Tim Manibusan

ILLUSTRATOR: Aliza Shalit

PHOTOGRAPHY COORDINATOR: Rachel Ackley

FRONT COVER PHOTOGRAPHY by Paula Shoultz

PHOTOGRAPHY by Paula Shoultz, unless otherwise noted

Published by Stash Books, an imprint of C&T Publishing, Inc., P.O. Box 1456,
Lafayette, CA 94549

Library of Congress Cataloging-in-Publication Data

Names: Lawson, Theresa M. (Theresa Marie), 1979- author.

Title: Hand-stitched oasis : embroider realistic elements; step-by-step

guide with 35 techniques / Theresa M. Lawson.

Description: Lafayette, CA : Stash Books, an imprint of C&T Publishing,

Inc., [2024] | Summary: "Learn how to hand stitch and capture the magic

of your own happy place with five projects, more than thirty

step-by-step techniques, and a pattern library to help you create an

embroidered oasis that is uniquely yours"-- Provided by publisher.

Identifiers: LCCN 2023035309 | ISBN 9781644034125 (trade paperback) | ISBN
9781644034132 (ebook)

Subjects: LCSH: Embroidery--Patterns. | Needlework.

Classification: LCC TT770 .L385 2024 | DDC 746.44041--dc23/eng/20231012

LC record available at https://lccn.loc.gov/2023035309

Printed in China

10 9 8 7 6 5 4 3 2 1

acknowledgments

You would not be reading this book without the village of people whose encouragement, talent, and downright hard work pushed it into existence to help elevate embroidery and needlework as a recognized art form. This sentiment is especially true of my editing team, Roxane Cerda and Karly Wallace, who worked (literally) day and night to keep the book moving forward when I wavered, encouraged me when I was unsure, and created when I felt burned out. With their input, the book developed into a better resource than I could ever have achieved alone.

Thanks also go to the C&T publishing team, whose work keeps crafting and creating available to audiences around the world.

Happy stitching!

contents

introduction

If you've spent much time in the Western world, you'll undoubtedly have heard the term *happy place*. It usually refers to a place, real or imaginary, where you can turn off your thoughts and breathe a sigh of contentment. Sometimes, it's a memory we can return to time and again when we need a dose of calm.

In this book, we bring your happy place from the back of your mind into the real world. When you've completed your project with this book, you'll have created a world that you can look at each day and feel that moment of calm whenever you need it.

This book focuses on a variety of outdoor happy places, ranging from desert scenes to cool mountaintop lakes. Happy places vary greatly between people, and you may find that particular objects or scenes that make you happy aren't included in this book. But with the tools in the following chapters, you'll be able to use the design process to create those objects on your own. As you create different happy places, your confidence will build. Eventually, you'll find yourself lost in a world of embroidery—not a bad place to be, if you ask me.

Are you ready? Then, let's begin!

before you dive in

If you're reading this chapter, great job! Many people would be tempted to skip this crucial step in getting the most out of this book and your embroidery project—but not you! Now, you'll know how to use each chapter to its fullest. *Hand-Stitched Oasis* will guide you step by step to bring your happy place to life.

You can do anything here—the only
prerequisite is that it makes you happy.

~ Bob Ross ~

What to Know Before You Start

Although stitchers of all skill levels can use *Hand-Stitched Oasis*, this book is not a "how to embroider" guide, although it does include instructions for many basic stitches. It may be useful to work on a small project first to practice some of the embroidery stitches you might be unfamiliar with. If you want to explore even more stitch options, check out *Hand Embroidery Dictionary*, by Christen Brown (C&T Publishing) and *Everyday Embroidery for Modern Stitchers*, by Megan Eckman (C&T Publishing).

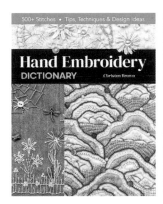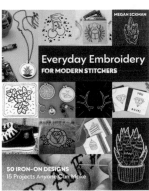

A Note About the Process

As you're building your happy place, try to think of your project as ongoing. Be fluid and easygoing as you bring your world to life. Add things to your world if you feel like they should be there and remove them if you don't feel like they're needed—even if that's not how it looks "in real life." This process is not paint by numbers—this world is yours and it can be whatever you want it to be. *Hand-Stitched Oasis* is as much about the process as it is about the end result.

The Path to Your Oasis

Creating your embroidered oasis involves the following steps:

DESIGN We work together to bring your vision out of your head and onto the canvas. We go through important elements to include, creating a pattern either from a photograph or your imagination, and we transfer that design to your fabric. Don't worry if you don't believe that you have artistic skills—we have a stash of mix-and-match patterns for you to trace or download and add to your design. To see the available patterns, flip to the Pattern Library (page 114).

STITCH This step is where the real fun begins—when you take needle to fabric! This chapter helps you bring your world to life as we walk through design tricks, stitches, and all-important techniques. The techniques section forms the bulk of the book for a reason! Here, you get to choose your favorite stitching technique for the element you are creating. As you add more techniques, you slowly start to see your world come to life!

FINISH Once you've committed your beautiful world to canvas, you'll obviously want to admire it for years to come. We go through some finishing techniques and suggestions for the placement of your finished piece, so you can be transported back to that world whenever you see your wonderful work of art.

TIP ⟋⟍⟋ *Tips throughout the book suggest ways you can get the most out of your embroidery or project. They are only suggestions, so take or leave what you find helpful.*

ready-to-stitch projects

But wait! That's not all this book has in store for you. The end of the book also includes ready-made designs, just in case you'd like a little practice before diving into creating your own (or if you just happen to like the designs).

materials

You don't need any special tools to start creating your happy place. If you've ever embroidered before, chances are you already have everything you need. If not, this opportunity is the perfect chance to find a new happy place (and one of my personal favorites)—your local needlework store! This section lists the items I recommend gathering before you get started. *Note: You choose embroidery floss colors later in the design process.*

Essential Materials

FABRIC You'll be embroidering a lot on your fabric, so you'll want something that can stand up to the stitching. Choose a strong fabric with a tight weave. Also, consider the scene that you are stitching: What kind of background color or canvas will complement your oasis? Does it feature a bright blue sky? Perhaps a light blue cotton fabric will help you capture that element. Is your oasis an old forest with knotted trees? Perhaps a textured linen will help you add character.

Some fabrics that lend themselves to embroidery are:

Linen: This tightly woven fabric is often used for soft furnishings in the home. Linen has been used as an embroidery surface for many years and it comes in many colors and textures. You can find linen at most, if not all, fabric and needlework stores.

Flax blend: A flax-linen blend is a mixture of cotton, linen, and rayon. It is similar to linen, except it often has a rougher texture. It is great to use if you want your canvas to have more texture or personality.

Cotton: Cotton is another common fabric in Western households. It is smoother, tighter, and thinner than linen. Cotton is great to use

if you want your canvas to disappear into the background. However, as this fabric tends to be thin, it does not stand up very well to heavy embroidery. If you choose cotton, consider doubling up your fabric or adding security to your fabric surface with a stabilizer.

Twill: Rather than the content of the fabric, *twill* refers to its weave. Twill is a wonderful fabric to use for embroidery. It provides an even, flat surface and is tightly woven, offering a strong base for your many stitches. It can be expensive, but if you are working on a large or complicated project, it can be worth the investment.

EMBROIDERY FRAME Embroidery hoops are probably the easiest and most widely available type of embroidery frames. You can also use them to frame your project when it's finished. If this project is your first, avoid bamboo embroidery hoops. They can flake, cause splinters, and are rough on your fabric. Instead, choose a strong and well-made hoop, such as one of polished beech.

I suggest starting with a 6″–10″ (15–25cm) or larger hoop so that you do not end up working in miniature!

If you aren't keen on a round scene, consider other frame options, including stretcher bars, slate frames, Q-Snap frames, and scroll frames. Unlike when using embroidery hoops, you'll have to remove the piece from the frame to finish and display it. Frames are more expensive, but they are also designed to hold up to the test of time and many hours of embroidering. They can be an investment, so talk to your local needlework store owner to find the one most suitable for your piece.

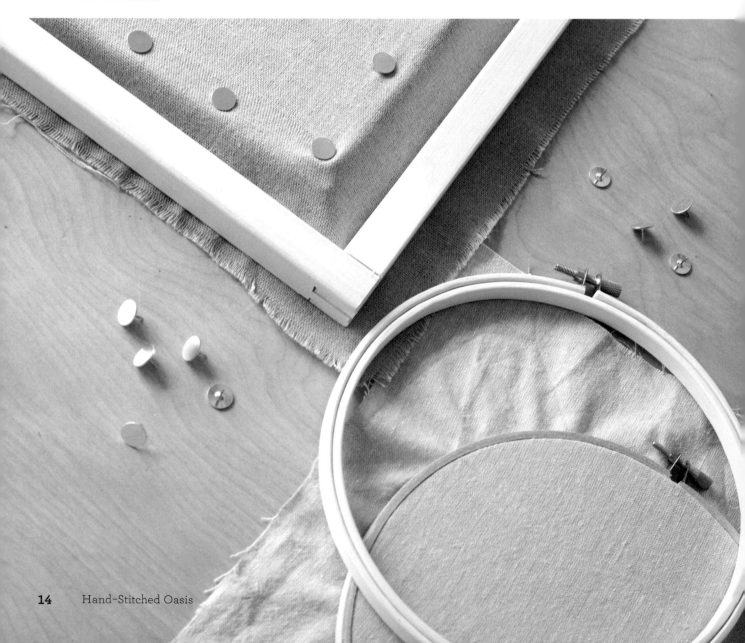

NEEDLE Just like frames, many types of needles are available for embroidery. Although each has a purpose, the one I get the most use from is a #8 crewel needle. These have an eye wide enough to handle a variety of threads and a point sharp enough to get through tough layers.

TRANSFER MATERIALS Just type *embroidery transfer* into your chosen search engine, and you'll be inundated with tools, methods, and tricks. Sticky transfer paper, transfer pencils, pens—the list is almost endless! The good thing about embroidering your happy place is that you'll likely be using a lot of stitches, which will cover up the remnants of any method that you use. In Transferring Your Design (page 79), you will choose a method that is easy and fun for you.

THREAD Many people could tell you that they have been bored to tears by my soliloquies on thread! I'll talk to anyone—or just the walls— about my favorite kinds and how to use them. Luckily, in you, I've found a listening ear! We dive more into the use of thread in Bringing Your Happy Place to Life (page 32), where we talk about how different types of thread can help you achieve different effects. Just wait until you see what metallic threads can do! Until then, just know that you'll be spoiled for choice in the types and colors of thread available for your oasis.

Embroidery floss: This thread is the most versatile type you can use. It is widely available online and in all needlework and craft stores. It comes in hundreds of colors and often in different materials, such as linen and metallic. One of the handiest aspects of embroidery floss is that it is made up of six individual strands, making it divisible. This trait can be invaluable when you want to capture details or depth by stitching with a thinner or thicker thread.

Crewel wool: Typically used for crewel or needlepoint, crewel wool is an indivisible thread that is most similar to knitting yarn, but slightly thinner. For projects like the ones in this book, it is best used when you'd like to add a thicker or more textured look to the object you're stitching. It works great for tree trunks!

Silk: Silk is a wonderful thread to use. It has a soft sheen and smooth texture, which can help it depict shiny objects. It can be expensive and tends to shred if drawn through the fabric too many times. To avoid this issue and get your money's worth, consider using shorter lengths of thread over smaller surface areas.

Metallic: Metallic thread comes in divisible and indivisible forms. It is shiny, stiff, and best

used for small objects or accents, as it often shreds and tangles easily due to its nature. Try using it sparingly in a lake or sea to depict sparkling waves.

Perle cotton: Perle (sometimes spelled *pearl*) is an indivisible thread. Its twisted nature gives it a ropelike appearance, which can be great if you want to capture a rippled surface such as a still lake or sand.

Sewing thread: Sewing thread is commonly used for clothing or quilting, and as such, is very strong and thin. It comes in a variety of colors and is quite affordable. For projects like the ones in this book, it can be used for couching (affixing another thread to the surface of your fabric), creating small details, or transferring your design (see Transferring Your Design, page 79).

PAINTS Yes, that's right—get your fabric paints ready because we'll be capturing some interesting effects with them. Check out Backgrounds (page 35) for more information.

FELT Wool felt in a 1mm thickness can be helpful when you want to add an appliqué element (see Appliqué, page 49). In addition, when you want an element to be subtly raised to appear closer to the viewer, you can add a layer of fiberfill padding underneath a layer of felt before adding your stitches (see Padding, page 50).

Things That Will Be Helpful

As you're trying to imagine what your happy place looks like, you may find some things helpful to use. Here is a list of optional items that can help you pull your dream world from your imagination and onto the canvas.

NOTEBOOK To keep track of your ideas and plan your embroidery, it's helpful to have a nice clean notebook dedicated to just this project. You can jot down ideas when inspiration hits and list all the techniques you plan to use and where. You can even use it to draft a quick sketch of your happy place before you make the design.

MOOD BOARD Mood boards can be so helpful in envisioning specific parts of your happy place. They can help you develop a bigger picture and get specific about what you want to include or what can be saved for future embroidery. You can go old school and place items on bulletin board with tacks, or you can simply dedicate a Pinterest board to your project and scroll through the website for inspiration.

PATTERN LIBRARY Lucky you! This book comes with an exclusive library of print-ready patterns designed to help you easily create and design your happy place! You can use the library items to build your happy place piece by piece, or you can mix and match individual elements with your own patterns. To see the available element patterns, check out the Pattern Library (page 114).

Original illustrations used to draft the pattern library

Lake DMC L995

Tree Trunk DMC 840

Tree Leaves

Painted Trees

Fabric = Deep Blue
(Sky)

6" Hoop

Painted

Water

design

Creating Your World

Before anything else, you need to design your oasis. Whether it is a real place or a place in your head, begin by asking yourself some questions:

- What type of outdoor scene do you envision?

- Is there water (a lake, river, or sea)?

- What's under your feet (grass, pebbles, sand, or something else)?

- What kinds of plants are there (tropical, forest trees, flowers, or other foliage)?

- Are there structures? If so, what are they?

All of these questions are important when designing and choosing how you will convey your happy place. Below, you'll answer those questions and start developing a clear image of your world so you can eventually create a pattern.

Optional: Building a Mood Board

Building a mood board can be a really helpful and fun exercise when starting to design your happy place.

Using your own photos: Whether they are physical photographs or images on your phone, you can use your own photos to create a mood board. Using your own images can really help transport you to the place you want to re-create. If you are a visual person, it can help to pull out or print inspiring images so you can move them around and group them. Pick an empty space on a wall or get yourself a magnetic board that you can stick photos to. Choose photos that contain a scene or an image that gives you that comforting feeling. On a sticky note or label, write one word that defines why that image appeals to you. Maybe it's *tree* or *autumn* or *seaside*. Make it something physical that you can include in your final design.

Using Images from the Internet: Perhaps your happy place isn't a place you've been, or, if it is, you have only memories but no photos. In this situation, the internet is your friend. You can perform a simple image search or try perusing the free section of a stock image website. If you want to re-create a specific place, search and find three images that define that place for you. If you don't have a specific place in mind, try doing an image search for a term that brings you comfort, such as *spacious* or *fresh* or *sunshine*. Find three images that really speak to you or feel like a place you'd be happy living in. Print the images or save them to a special album on your device.

Using Pinterest: Pinterest is a website and app that can be an incredible source of inspiration for your design. As with the previous options, you can search and pin inspirational images to a virtual mood board you create on Pinterest. Within the app, you'll find all kinds of images, or "pins," that you can add to your mood board. If you're someone who likes lists and color-coded sticky notes, a Pinterest mood board may be the way to go. You can even categorize your mood board within Pinterest! Some suggestions include "Colors I Like," "Plants I Like," or "Forest Scenes." Keep a shortcut or link to your Pinterest mood board so you can refer to it often.

Your Design Development Worksheet

Regardless of whether you choose to create a mood board, a Design Development Worksheet can help you decide what your design will look like. It also has the added benefit of keeping the inspiration alive and helping you track your work. Answer the questions in the worksheet on the form below or in a separate notepad. In the next section, you'll use your answers to flesh out your world!

If you don't wish to write in this book or if you plan to make a number of projects, you can also download and print a copy of this worksheet. To access the worksheet through the tiny URL, type the web address provided below into your browser window. Print directly from the browser window or download the worksheet. ▶ **tinyurl.com/11559-patterns-download**

the place that brings me comfort

What is your happy outdoor scene? _____

What kind of climate is it? Is it warm or cool? Sunny or snowy? _____

Is water there? Are waves lapping at your feet? _____

_____

_____

What plants or trees do you see? _____

_____

_____

What's under your feet? Grass? Sand? Pebbles? Snow? _____

_____

_____

What's in the background? Is it day or night? What's in the sky? Are there mountains, trees, an ocean?

_____

_____

_____

What colors do you see the most? Burgundy? Green? Brown? Yellow? Blue?

_____

_____

_____

Are there any major objects? A big oak tree? A marsh? _____

_____

_____

Putting It All Together: How to Design Your Happy Place

Now, it's time to take the inspiration you have gathered so far and start creating your design! The first step is to identify, scale, and sketch the important elements in your design. How you approach this step varies, depending on whether you are working from an inspiration photo or your imagination.

method 1: working from a photo or photos

You can create your design from a single or several photos. All you need to know are the major elements (objects) within the photo you want to re-create. If it's the whole photo image, great! You've got a ready-made pattern just waiting for you to resize and trace, following the Instructions for Building Your Design (page 30)! If you're using several photos, choose what you like most about each photo and include it in your design. If you created a photo mood board, refer to the defining words you chose for each photograph (see Optional: Building a Mood Board, page 22). Those are the objects you are going to take from those photos and place in your design.

CHOOSING THE MOST IMPORTANT OBJECTS

If you have created a mood board with photos, you may already have chosen the most important objects from them. If so, move on to Resizing (page 26).

If you are not yet sure what you want to include, lay your inspirational photos out before you. What about these photos do you like? Does something truly encompass what your happy place is? For example, it could be a giant oak tree that reminds you of the tree you used to climb at your grandparents' house. In another photo, maybe it's the fluffy white clouds.

When choosing the most important elements, try to think physically. It's easy to get caught up in the "mood" of your happy place, but it's really hard to stitch a concept, like *childhood*, or *summertime*. Instead, concentrate the what physical parts of the photo that inspire mood in you. The grass? The sky? The color?

When you have decided on the most important parts of the photo or photos you want to include, add any that you haven't already included to your Design Development Worksheet.

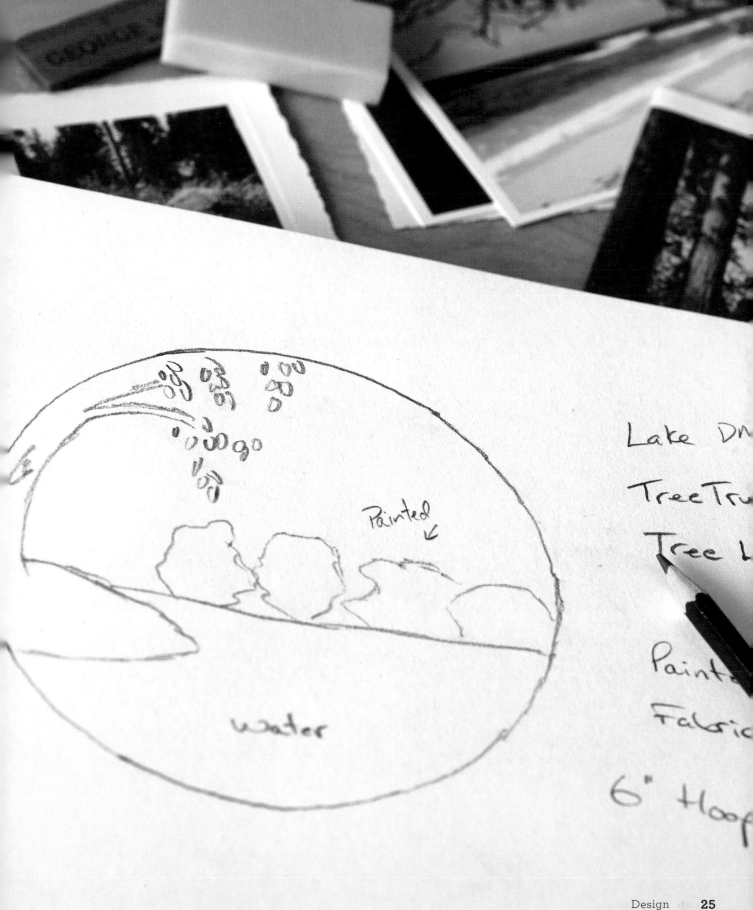

Lake Dr[...]

Tree Tru[...]

Tree L[...]

Painted

Fabric[...]

6" Hoop[...]

Painted

water

RESIZING

You may need to resize your photo(s) so the objects you will eventually stitch are at the size you want to stitch them. You'll then trace over the objects to create your design. If one of your photos depicts something that is not physical, such as a color, put the photo to one side, but keep it accessible.

The size of the photo(s) you need depends on the size you want your final piece to be. I recommend keeping the whole embroidery piece no smaller than 6˝ (15cm) and no larger than 12˝ (30cm). If it's any smaller, you'll run the risk of having to work at fairy sizes; if it's any larger, you'll have a hard time filling the space. Remember, you'll want to resize the photo so that the **object** you want to stitch is proportional and will fit with other objects in your final embroidered piece.

Keep in mind that not every object in your embroidery design will be the same scale. Objects in the distance will need to be reduced to a smaller size, and objects in the foreground will need to be larger. This detail will help you imply distance and achieve perspective in your finished embroidery piece.

To resize a photo to the measurement you want, scan it into your computer or take a digital photo so you have an editable JPEG file. I always use a word-processing program, such as Microsoft Word, to resize my JPEGs. In this type of program, I can insert the photo into a document and resize it to exactly the measurement I want before printing.

TIP *You may need to rotate the image to achieve the right size.*

method 2 : working from your imagination

When you're not working from physical images, it can be a little more difficult, but certainly not impossible, to form your design. Think of it as your unlimited power to create your own world!

I'm a big fan of meditation. Sometimes, a meditation teacher will ask you to imagine yourself in a happy place. My happy place is usually a place I've never been to—or that even exists! I just know that I can hear a stream nearby, I can feel moss under my seat, and I can hear leaves rustling.

To help create this world, refer to your Design Development Worksheet (page 23).

If you've filled in the worksheet, you should already have an image forming in your head of what your happy place looks like. If not, you may want to go back and fill it in now. It will be helpful, I promise.

CHOOSING WHAT TO INCLUDE

When working from your imagination, you don't need to include every object that you wrote down on your Design Development Worksheet. You really only need the objects that will convey the message of this comforting place. In my meditation example, I could include all kinds of plants, boulders, trees, a roaring waterfall in the background, birds in the trees, and mountains on the horizon, but doing so would turn my happy place into a busy world. The most important objects of my happy place are moss on the ground, a small stream cutting through the moss, and a tree overhead. They are simple and calm, the perfect way to bring my happy place to life.

When choosing what to include, think about the things that are the most important to your space. Weed out anything that's not absolutely necessary.

At the end of the book is the Pattern Library (page 114), which includes common objects that you may like to include in your design. If none of the objects included pique your interest, don't be afraid to draw them as you imagine them or use the photo method. **You don't have to be an artist; all you are looking for is a simple outline for your embroidery.** The stitches will do most of the work.

Photo by Hans/Pixabay

SIZING

The objects in the Pattern Library are designed to fit with each other within a 10˝ (25cm) embroidery piece. If you are creating a 10˝ (25cm) piece, you can copy the page you require as is. Keep in mind that not every object in your embroidery design will be the same scale. Objects in the distance will need to be reduced to a smaller size, and objects in the foreground will need to be larger. This variation will help you imply distance and achieve perspective in your finished embroidery piece. Should you need a larger or smaller size, download the image you need and insert it into a word-processing program. Then, follow the instructions in Resizing (page 26) to size it to the desired measurement.

This part is exciting because you will slowly watch your world come to life. Although you don't need to create a very detailed design, I recommend at the very least including a few outlines of the major aspects of your design—for example, where the land meets the sea or sky, any major structures, and trees or bushes.

To get started, gather a few items:

- A roll or several sheets of tracing paper

- A sketching pencil

- Your Design Development Worksheet

- Inspiration photo or photos of a scene you want to re-create to refer to as needed (optional)

instructions for building your design

By this point, you have resized your photo(s) and/or chosen the patterns you want to include. Next, you'll trace over these objects:

1 Secure your patterns or photo to a lightbox or window. Layer your tracing paper on top of your patterns or photo. Trace around each chosen object. Leave 1˝ (2.5cm) or so around each object you trace.

2 Take another piece or length of tracing paper that is the size of your final design. Draw a line to represent the horizon.

3 Place each object where it appears in relation to your horizon line. Working from the background to the foreground, trace each of the objects you traced previously onto the new piece of tracing paper.

4 When you have a full scene you are happy with, write down any concepts included on the Design Development Worksheet or your mood board on the tracing paper design—for example, autumn leaves for the tree or pink sky behind clouds.

5 Read through your Design Development Worksheet and make sure that you have included everything you want.

There it is—your happy place! You can use this paper as your pattern or simply as a reference when stitching.

bringing your happy place to life

Capturing Depth

One of the best ways to bring your happy place to life is to insert depth into your piece. Inserting depth means that when the viewer looks at your finished piece, they'll see the illusion of shadows and distance. There are several ways to capture depth, and I outline a few here. Try to combine these in your piece to make your happy place really stand out.

use color

You'll notice when collecting your materials that embroidery threads come in a rainbow of colors. You can use this variety to your advantage when creating depth. When selecting colors for your project, think about whether the object you will be stitching will cast a shadow or will have a textured surface. Either of these means that you will likely need three shades of the same color to capture depth for that object.

For example, let's say that you are embroidering a tree. If you weren't worried about depth, you would choose one brown color for the trunk and one green color for the leaves. But in real life, the tree trunk alone has many different colors. Why? Because it is a textured surface. When stitching the tree trunk, you will be stitching dimples or holes in the tree with a darker shade, while parts of the tree that capture the sun will be a much lighter shade.

One easy way to capture depth, especially for a textured surface like a tree trunk, is to combine threads. This effect is best achieved with stranded embroidery floss because you can combine strands of different colors. Stitching with two or three different colors of floss in one length of thread will naturally provide you with a dappled shade effect, regardless of the stitching technique you choose!

use thread weight

Varying thread weight is a great way to capture depth in your embroidered piece. By simply changing the thickness of your thread, you can make objects in your happy place appear closer or farther away.

Threads come in different weights; the higher the number, the thinner it is. For example, say that you wanted to depict a bush very close up to the viewer—you might choose a perle cotton #5 thread. However, if you wanted to stitch several bushes far away, a #5 thread would be too thick. You would instead choose a #12 thread, making your stitches naturally smaller and, thus, appearing to be farther away!

The exception to this technique is stranded floss, but it is even easier to use to reflect depth—simply use fewer strands the farther away your object is from the viewer. Take a brick wall for example. You might use all six strands for a very close wall. However, with walls in the background, you might only use one or two strands together.

adding padding

Layering material on top of your embroidery fabric before stitching on top will add additional depth to the element being embroidered. You can achieve this look by tacking a layer of fiberfill under a layer of felt if you want all or a portion of an element to be raised (see Padding, page 50).

layering

Layering is a very natural way to capture depth in any scene you might stitch. It is the act of arranging one object in front of another. When creating your pattern, you did this by placing objects on your tracing paper from the background to the foreground. As you stitch your oasis, you will work the same way.

Starting with objects that appear in the background of your piece allows you to easily layer one over the other without having to stitch around larger objects. By working this way, you will capture depth in your piece without really trying!

backgrounds

To take some of the legwork out of creating depth in your portrait, you can exploit the background of your piece. Here are three easy ways to manipulate the background of your embroidery piece to help you capture depth.

USE PAINT

Fabric paints come in an array of colors, and using them in embroidery has become commonplace. You don't need to be a great artist to use paint in your embroidery—just include a few subtle hints of distant objects to give the effect of depth.

If you choose to add paint to hint at your background, do so before adding any embroidery. Make sure that your fabric is prepared and stretched in your frame before you start. You don't need a lot of paint on your paintbrush—mix in a little water if your paint is too thick. Let your background fully dry before you start stitching.

Ideas: Try adding a few fluffy clouds to your sky by dabbing light gray patches with the paintbrush. Experiment and be creative! For instructions on painting clouds, including which paints and brushes to use, see Painted Clouds (page 53). Once you become confident in creating painted clouds, you can use the same technique to suggest distant trees. Maybe try using a wide brush to swipe paint across the canvas to create a magenta sunset or try creating a dappled sun effect by dabbing light green and yellow spots all over the background.

USE FABRIC COLORS

Try choosing a base fabric the same color as the background you envision. Choose a blue fabric to depict a wide blue sky or a deep green to reflect a cool, dark forest. Hand-dyed fabrics can have a wonderfully random, swirly pattern that can mimic cloudy skies or a starry galaxy.

MAKE SUBTLE HINTS

Choose an object in the room you're in right now and focus on it for five seconds. You'll notice that you can only see the detail of what you're focusing on. Everything in the periphery of your vision is just blurry, general shapes. That's an effect you can use to help capture depth in your embroidery piece.

For objects that are not in the forefront of your design, all you need to concentrate on is capturing their **general color** and their **general shape**. Leave all the detail work for objects that sit closer to the viewer.

For example, perhaps in your background, you have a dense forest of trees. In real life, you wouldn't be able to distinguish the detail of each individual tree—you would just be able to pick out shades of green and a few distant trunks here and there. In this case, you might take a single strand of dark brown thread and randomly place short vertical straight stitches on top of a wall of painted tree canopies. This technique will depict the dense forest without stealing attention from what is in front.

Selecting Supplies for Your Project

Before you start stitching, think about the types of materials you'll need for your project. You will need to choose materials based on the decisions you've made about your design so far.

❋ NOTE ❋

You will see suggested colors and thread types in Stitching Your Elements (page 52). Please use these as suggestions only—color choice in particular is an easy way to express your creativity.

When selecting your fabric, consider whether you want your fabric to reflect the background in any way (see Use Fabric Colors, above) or whether you want a plain background so your stitches shine. Refer to Materials (page 12) to decide which kind of fabric will help you do this. How big is your happy place? Do you need a lot of fabric, or will a sample size

suffice? In general, you will need a piece of fabric that with at least an extra 2″ (5cm) on all sides to allow for placement in the hoop or frame. For example, if you select a 10″ (25cm) hoop, you will need a piece of fabric that is at least 14″ × 14″ (36 × 36cm). It is best to allow yourself a little bit extra.

To choose your threads, make note of the thread weights you'll need for each of your objects (see Use Thread Weight, page 34). Do you have any tiny objects, or are they all on the same visual plane, making thread weight a nonissue? And don't forget about thread color! Will you need a few different shades to capture depth in certain objects (see Use Color, page 33)?

So many thread colors are available to you. It can be overwhelming to go to the store and see everything all at once. This moment is when a color card can be useful. Color cards list all the available thread colors and types from a supplier. You can then simply make a list of the colors you need and head to the store. Color cards can be easily bought online from any needlework supplier.

Think about whether you will need any other materials. Will you be painting your background (see Use Paint, page 35)? If so, which colors will you need? Do you intend to add padded areas?

selecting for texture and effect

When choosing materials, it's also important to consider what kind of texture or effect the material can lend to your embroidery piece. Different types of material can cut down on some of the work you'll need to do because they already capture aspects of the object you are embroidering. Take our tree bark example:

You can also combine different threads! For example, if I am embroidering a serene lake, I might combine a silky blue thread with a shiny metallic thread to capture the rippled and reflective surface of the water.

By choosing a wool thread to embroider my tree trunk, I can capture the rough, textured quality of the trunk.

basic stitches and techniques to choose from

Stitching Your Elements (page 52), includes suggested stitches for each technique. Here are the stitches you should get to know. If you are unfamiliar with any of them, try practicing them on a separate piece of fabric until you are comfortable.

Basic Stitches

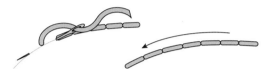

1 Bring your thread up from the back of the fabric (A) and then plunge the needle through to the back, one stitch length to the right (B). Bring the thread back up to the top of the fabric, one stitch length to the left of the original stitch (C).

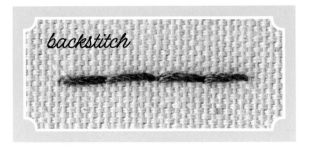

2 Plunge the needle down at the beginning of your previous stitch (A) and then bring the needle, up one stitch length to the left (D) of point (C).

3 Repeat.

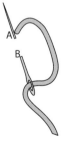

1 Bring your thread to the front of the fabric (A) and then plunge your needle through to the back, one stitch length (or however long you want your knot to be) away (B). Bring your need back up through the first hole, but don't pull the needle all the way through.

2 Wrap your thread around the needle however many times it takes for the wrapped thread to reach the length of your stitch (a little more, if you want a loopy effect).

3 Pull your needle through the wrapped loops and fold the looped stitch down over to the beginning point of the stitch (B). Bring your needle back through to the back of the fabric to finish the stitch.

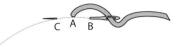

chain stitch

1 Bring your needle to the front of the fabric (A). Take your needle back through, just next to the original stitch (B), and pull your thread through, but not all the way. Leave a loop that is about an inch long. Bring the needle back to the front of the fabric, one stitch length away (C), making sure to go through the loop you just made.

2 Pull the thread until the loop catches at the bottom of your thread. This is your first chain stitch. To make more, just repeat the process.

3 To finish, bring your thread up through the fabric, as though you are going to start another loop. Instead, plunge your needle over your last chain stitch to secure it (D).

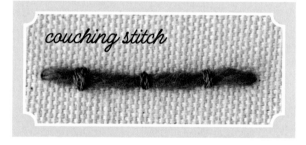

couching stitch

Couching is an easy way to depict a wiggly line. It is best to couch large threads, such as wool, string, or ribbon. Use a sewing thread as your couching thread.

1 Draw a guiding line where you want the couched thread.

2 Secure your sewing thread to your fabric at the starting point of your couching line with a couple of tiny stitches.

3 Bring the thread you wish to couch up just above your sewing thread. You may need to snip a small hole in the weave of the fabric if your couch thread is very thick.

4 Lay your couch thread along your guiding line and make small stitches over the thread with your sewing thread to secure it in place. Keep your securing stitches at least ¼″ (6mm) apart.

5 When you come to the end of your guiding line, make your last securing stitch.

6 Follow by plunging your couched thread through your fabric and securing it on the back of your work.

*detached chain
(lazy daisy) stitch*

1 Bring your needle and thread up through your fabric at your starting point (A). Plunge the needle back down right next to your starting point (B), leaving a loose loop (do not pull the thread all the way through).

2 Bring your needle back up through the fabric a short distance from your starting point, making sure to go through the loop you just made (C). The distance you choose to bring your needle up will determine the length of the detached chain stitch.

3 Pull the thread through until you create a petal-shaped loop. Secure the detached chain stitch by plunging the needle through the fabric slightly below your catch thread, creating a securing stitch (D).

fern stitch

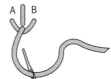

1 Make a vertical straight stitch. Bring your needle up to the left of your straight stitch, about half way down and a half stitch length across (A). Bring your needle back down through the fabric at the same level, but to the right of your straight stitch (B). Bring the needle up at the bottom of your straight stitch and above the loop between A and B.

2 Pull the thread through until you make a short V shape with the loop thread. Make another vertical stitch about the same length as the one above.

3 Repeat steps 1 and 2 until you have reached the length you want your fern stitch to be.

You can vary the width of your V shape to create a widening tree or fern shape.

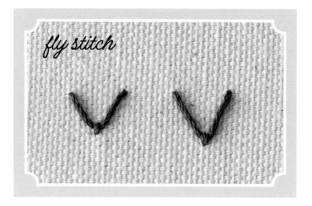

fly stitch

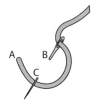

1 Bring your needle and thread up at your starting point (A). Take your needle down a stitch length away or the width that you want your fly stitch wings to be (B). Pull the thread through (but not all the way through), leaving a loose loop. Bring your needle back up through the fabric, just below the two points of your loop (C), catching the loop thread (the loop thread should be below your needle). Where you choose to bring your needle up will determine the height of the fly stitch.

2 Pull the thread through until you create a V shape out of the loop thread. Secure the fly stitch by plunging the needle through the fabric slightly below your catch thread (D), creating a securing stitch.

french knot

1 Bring your needle and thread up through the fabric (A). Hold the working thread taut with your free hand. Place the needle on top of your working thread, about ½˝ (12mm) from the fabric. Wrap the thread around your needle twice and pull it taut. Keep your waste thread away from your stitch.

2 While holding the thread wraps taut on the needle, plunge the needle through your fabric at the same point (but not the same hole) as your starting point.

 **3** Keep the thread fairly taut as you pull the needle to the back of the fabric so your thread wraps do not unravel as you create your knot. Do not pull the thread too hard, or your knot will disappear to the back of your fabric.

granitos stitch

1 Make a vertical straight stitch that is the length you want your granitos stitch to be. Bring your needle back up to the front of the fabric through the same hole you made when beginning your straight stitch (A).

 **2** Plunge your needle back down through the same hole at the bottom of your straight stitch (B). As you pull the thread taut, nudge the new stitch so that it lies to one side of the original straight stitch.

3 Bring your needle back up through the first hole you made (A) and back down through the bottom of the stitch (B). As you pull the thread taut, nudge the new stitch so that it lies to the other side of the original straight stitch.

4 Repeat until the stitch has reached the desired size/width, usually two or three stitches.

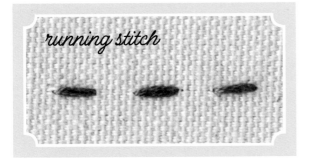

running stitch

1 Bring your needle and thread up through the fabric (A). Plunge the needle down through the fabric, one stitch length away (B), and then back up to the top of the fabric, one stitch farther (C).

 **2** Repeat until you have placed the desired number of stitches.

satin stitch

1 Bring your thread to the front of your fabric at one end of the area you want to cover with satin stitches. Plunge the needle down on the opposite side of the shape where you began.

2 Make your next stitch just as you did the first, right next to the first stitch. Continue along until you have covered the whole area.

TIP ⟳ *The key is to make your stitches lay flat:*

- *Use only one strand of thread.*

- *Try using a fabric with a tight weave or backing your fabric with one in a tight weave.*

- *If you are not confident with the stitch yet, try starting in the middle of the area you want to cover and moving outward.*

- *Before you begin to satin stitch, pad the area you would like to cover with a layer of long and short straight stitches to add stability to your satin stitches.*

seed stitch

1 Bring the needle up at your starting point and then bring it down a stitch length away. The stitch should be no more than a scant ⅛˝ (2mm) in length.

2 Add additional seed stitches randomly until you fill the desired area or achieve the intended effect.

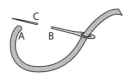

1 Bring the needle up at your starting point (A) and back down through the fabric, one longer stitch length away (B). Do not pull the thread all the way through, leaving a larger loop of thread. Holding the thread loop below your line of stitches, bring the needle back up halfway between your stitch start and end (C).

2 Pull the thread to tighten your stitch. Take the needle down one regular stitch length away from the end point of your first stitch (D). Bring the needle up at the end of your previous stitch (in the middle of the start and end of your current stitch). Continue until your line of stem stitches is as long as desired.

TIP ⌒⌒ *Be sure to consistently hold the thread loop to the same side to achieve the desired twisted look of stem stitches.*

- -

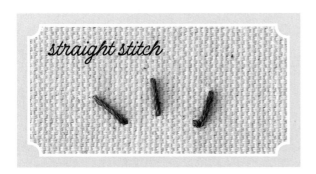

Bring the needle up at your starting point (A). Bring the needle down a stitch length away (B).

A straight stitch can be any length you need.

tack (basting) stitch

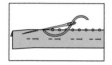

1 Bring your needle and thread up through the fabric. Plunge the needle down through the fabric layers, one stitch length away, and then bring it back up to the top of the fabric, one stitch farther away.

2 Continue until the two pieces of fabric are held together.

TIP ⌒ Don't Limit Yourself

You might like to use many embroidery stitches out there for your oasis. Type embroidery stitches *into a search engine and click on the Images tab to browse through them.*

The table on the next two pages gives you some ideas for how to employ the stitches you just learned. It shows how I tend to use the basic stitches and which techniques use which stitches. In addition, you will find a list of the stitches I would use for each aspect of the various motifs in the Pattern Library. Remember, though, that these are always just ideas and suggestions. Use the information in the table as a jumping off point and explore using the various stitches in new ways!

stitch applications

Stitches	I Use This For	Associated Techniques	Associated Pattern Library Motifs
Back Stitch	Outlines, plant stems		Camper outline, tent outline, bridge, vine stem
Bullion Knot	Reed seed head, pumpkins	Pudgy Pumpkin fruit (page 74), Reeds (page 72)	
Chain Stitch	Cactus	Cactus (page 69)	Cactus
Couching Stitch	Snow, long flowing lines	Snow (page 58)	
Detached Chain (Lazy Daisy) Stitch	Leaves, large petals, foliage	Oak or Maple Tree, canopy (page 66), Tulip leaves (page 71), Daisy petals (page 72), Potted Plant foliage (page 73)	Vine leaf, sprout, potted plant, tulip, tree canopy
Fern Stitch	Small plants, distant trees, palm leaves	Palm Tree fronds (page 67), Floral and Small Plants (page 70)	Tumbleweed, willow tree canopy, fern, pine tree canopy
Fly Stitch	Birds	Birds (page 55)	
French Knot	Earth, bushes, wave foam, flowers	Waves (page 62), Bushes or Shrubs (page 69), Lavender flowers (page 71), Daisy centers (page 72)	Bush, tree canopy, waterfall plunge pool, lavender
Granitos Stitch	Pebbles or rocks, tulips	River Pebbles (page 59), Tulip flowers (page 71)	Tulip
Running Stitch	Design transfer, embroidery hoop backing techniques		
Satin Stitch	Large bodies of water, sand, tree trunks, filling large spaces, brick or stone	Beach Sand (page 58), Palm Tree trunk (page 67), Potted Plant terra-cotta pot (page 73)	Shed, barn, or structure; stairs; dock, boat, and seacraft; fountain; watering can; camper fill-in; tent fill-in; picnic basket; plateau fill-in; gazebo roof; stone wall; oar or paddle; blanket; plant pot

Stitches	I Use This For	Associated Techniques	Associated Pattern Library Motifs
Seed Stitch	Tree canopies, earth, stars	Stars (page 55), Earth or Fallen Leaves (page 59), Meandering Pathway (page 60), Distant Trees or Shrubs (page 63)	Tree canopy, bush, pathway
Stem Stitch	Tree bark, sun, moving water	Sun and Moon (page 54), Lake or Sea (page 61), Oak or Maple Tree trunk (page 65)	Fallen log/driftwood, tree stump, birdbath, picnic bench, fire-pit logs, tree trunk, waterfall, plateau outline, shed or barn walls, picket fence, dock
Straight Stitch	Stems, stalks, very distant pine trees, grass, structures	Grassy Meadow (page 56), Waves (page 62), Pine Tree (page 64), Floral and Small Plant stems (page 70), Lavender stems (page 71), Tulip stems (page 71), Daisy stems (page 72), Reed stems (page 72), Potted Plant stalk (page 73), Pudgy Pumpkin stem (page 74), Brick (page 76), Stone (page 76), Lumber Plank (page 77)	Distant pine trees to fill a mountain shape, seating, rail fence, gazebo, trellis, dock, swing set, fire, oar handles, lighthouse
Tack/Tacking (Basting) Stitch	Design transfer, appliqué	Appliqué Hill (page 57), Boulder (page 60), Pudgy Pumpkin base (page 74)	
Appliqué	Boulders, distant mountains	Appliqué Hill (page 57), Boulder (page 60), Pudgy Pumpkin base (page 74)	
Padding	Pumpkins	Pudgy Pumpkin shape (page 74)	

Basic Techniques

appliqué

For appliqué on embroidery, it is often preferable to use a fabric that will not fray, such as wool felt.

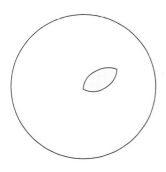

1 Cut out the shape of your appliqué piece from your appliqué fabric and place the appliqué piece on your base fabric in the position you want it to be secured.

2 Make very small tack stitches (see Tack [Basting] Stitch, page 46) along the edge of your appliqué fabric to secure the appliqué to your base fabric.

TIP ⁓ *If you are using a lightweight fabric, such as quilting cotton, you may want to cut out a slightly larger appliqué piece so that you are able to fold the edges under as you secure it to your base fabric. This method will provide you with a clean edge that does not fray.*

padding

You can add padding underneath your stitches by tacking a layer of fiberfill under a layer of felt on top of the area to be stitched, creating raised stitches.

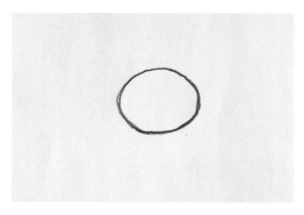

1 On tracing paper, outline the entire area to be padded.

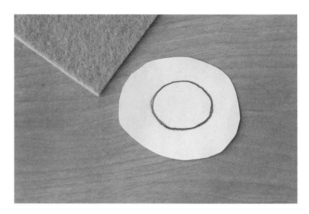

2 Cut out around the shape you just drew, leaving a 1˝ (2.5cm) margin around the shape.

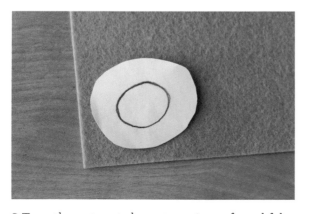

3 Tape the cut-out shape to a piece of wool felt.

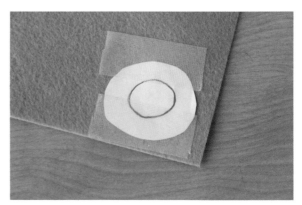

4 Cut along the lines through the paper and the felt.

5 Place your felt shape on your fabric.

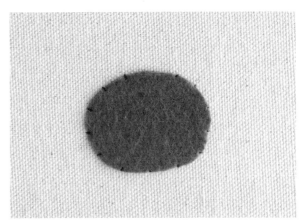

6 Using hand-sewing thread and a hand-sewing needle, make tiny tack stitches around your felt shape, leaving ³⁄₁₆˝ (5mm) between each stitch (see Tack [Basting] Stitch, page 46). Leave ³⁄₈˝ (1cm) of space between your first and last tack stitch.

7 Gently stuff a small amount of fiberfill underneath your secured felt through the largest gap between your tack stitches. Add more stuffing as needed to achieve the desired depth. (Do not overfill the area, as it will make subsequent stitching more difficult.)

8 Close the stuffing hole with an additional tack stitch.

You can add more layers of padding where greater depth is needed.

stitching your elements

Think of the techniques section as a buffet: You select from the available dishes and add each to your plate. When you sit down to eat, you have a full plate. Choose from the following elements for instruction on embroidering each of the objects in your design. By the time you have completed all the elements on your canvas, you will have a full embroidery piece!

Look through this chapter and select the technique for each of the objects in your design. It may help to note on your pattern or Design Development Worksheet which technique you are choosing for each object in your pattern and the page number.

Sky

painted clouds

RECOMMENDED SUPPLIES

White or light gray fabric paint

Round-headed paintbrush

Blue background fabric

INSTRUCTIONS

1 Prepare your fabric in the frame, making sure that it's drum-tight.

2 Wet your paintbrush and squeeze out excess water.

3 Add a small amount of paint to the tip of your paintbrush.

4 Gently dab the paint onto the fabric in a cloudlike shape. No need to be precise—clouds aren't precise shapes.

5 Allow to dry for 24 hours before stitching over.

TIPS

Add Depth

Add depth to your painted clouds by swirling a drop of dark gray paint into the white. Do not mix in thoroughly.

Distant Trees

Rather than clouds, use this same technique to create distant trees. Simply swap the white or light gray fabric paint for green fabric paint.

sun and moon

RECOMMENDED SUPPLIES

2 strands of silver (for moon) or 2 strands of gold (for sun) metallic thread

RECOMMENDED STITCH

Stem stitch

INSTRUCTIONS

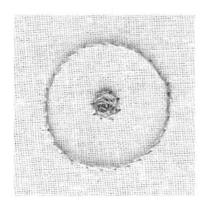

1 Create a circle shape on your canvas where you would like your sun by drawing around a bottle cap or coin. Stitch the circle with stem stitch.

2 Make a small securing stitch in the center of the circle with your thread.

3 Starting in the center and working in a spiral, make stem stitches within the circle until you have filled the shape.

4 Fill any bare patches with additional stem stitches.

TIP ⌒ *Switching from day to night is as simple as changing the color of your fabric and thread! Dark fabrics with silver thread convey the moon at nighttime, whereas a bright background with gold thread says daylight.*

TIP ⌒ *Metallic thread can be quite difficult to work with. Avoid frustration by working with shorter-than-normal lengths of thread, approximately 6˝ (15cm). Thread conditioner or wax can help create a smoother glide and to prevent shedding.*

RECOMMENDED SUPPLIES

1–2 strands of black embroidery floss

RECOMMENDED STITCH

Fly stitch

INSTRUCTIONS

1 Create a small fly stitch with a short width. Your fly stitches will need to be small to depict distant birds.

2 Create four or five more birds with fly stitches, varying the height and width of the birds' wingspans.

TIP ⌇ *Switch one or two strands to convey birds that are at different distances from the viewer.*

RECOMMENDED SUPPLIES

2 strands of white-gold metallic thread
Dark blue or black background fabric

RECOMMENDED STITCH

Seed stitch

INSTRUCTIONS

1 Create randomized seed stitches all across your sky area.

2 Cross some of the seed stitches over one another to depict sparkling stars.

TIP ⌇ *Consider using metallic sewing thread for a more subtle star effect or silver sequins for a more dramatic effect.*

Meadows, Fields, and Grassy Spaces

RECOMMENDED SUPPLIES

1 strand of very light pistachio-green embroidery floss

1 strand of medium green embroidery floss

1 strand of dark green embroidery floss

RECOMMENDED STITCH

Straight stitch

INSTRUCTIONS

1 Randomly straightstitch varying lengths of your dark green embroidery floss across the meadow area of your canvas. Allow some stitches to overlap and others to be at a distance. Try not to be too uniform, but remember that longer straight stitches should be towards the front and shorter toward the back to add perspective to your piece.

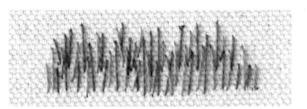

2 Repeat the process with the medium and then the light green embroidery floss.

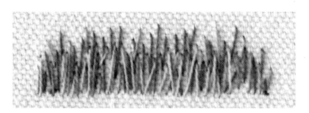

3 Repeat steps 1 and 2 until your meadow area is filled.

TIP ◠◡◟ *Change the thread colors to varying shades of yellow to depict a wheat field!*

appliqué hill

RECOMMENDED
SUPPLIES

Green 1mm-thick felt

Green sewing thread

RECOMMENDED STITCH

Appliqué

INSTRUCTIONS

1. Cut a sloping hill shape out of your felt. Make sure that it is large enough to cover the hill area on your canvas.

2. Position the felt hill on the canvas.

3. Make very small stitches and tack the felt into position with sewing thread.

TIP ⌒~⊙ *Think back to the lesson on layering (page 35). It may be easier to cut out a hill shape that is slightly larger than your canvas and position it over your base fabric so it can be secured with the embroidery hoop. This option will allow you to stitch objects in the foreground over your felt, adding depth to the piece.*

Snow, Sand, Pebbles, Earth, Pathway, and Boulders

RECOMMENDED SUPPLIES

DMC ECRU tapestry wool

White sewing thread

RECOMMENDED STITCH

Couching

INSTRUCTIONS

1 In descending rows, horizontally couch the tapestry wool across the snow area of your canvas.

2 Alternate the placement of the couch thread to convey drifts in the snow with the bulges of the tapestry wool.

TIP *For less fluffy snow drifts, try using a heavyweight perle cotton. A silk variety provides extra sheen.*

RECOMMENDED SUPPLIES

1 strand of ecru embroidery floss

1 strand of light beige embroidery floss

1 strand of beige embroidery floss

RECOMMENDED STITCH

Satin stitch

INSTRUCTIONS

1 Build the beach entirely with a long-stranded satin stitch.

2 Combine all three strands of your embroidery floss.

3 Start at the top of your beach area and work your way down.

4 If the area is more than 3˝ (8cm) wide, make additional stitches along the same row so that the stitches don't loosen while you work on the piece.

river pebbles

Alternate the thickness and width of your granitos stitch pebbles to convey a more natural scene.

RECOMMENDED SUPPLIES

1 strand of light-gray embroidery floss

1 strand of brown-gray embroidery floss

1 strand of silver-gray embroidery floss

RECOMMENDED STITCH

Granitos stitch

INSTRUCTIONS

1 Combine all three strands of your embroidery floss.

2 Make a granitos stitch for each individual pebble.

3 Create groups of pebbles in some places and scattered pebbles in other places.

earth or fallen leaves

TIP *Swap one of your medium brown embroidery floss colors for an orange embroidery floss to depict fallen leaves.*

RECOMMENDED SUPPLIES

6 strands of dark brown embroidery floss

6 strands of medium brown embroidery floss

6 strands of a different medium brown embroidery floss

RECOMMENDED STITCH

Seed stitch

INSTRUCTIONS

1 Starting with the dark brown embroidery floss, place random seed stitches across the area of earth on your canvas.

2 Repeat with both of the medium brown embroidery flosses.

3 Repeat steps 1 and 2 until your earth area is filled.

RECOMMENDED SUPPLIES

4–6 strands of medium taupe embroidery floss

4–6 strands of dark taupe embroidery floss

4–6 strands of light taupe embroidery floss

RECOMMENDED STITCH

Seed stitch

INSTRUCTIONS

1 Lightly draw your pathway guidelines. Try not to use a method that will stand out too much or cannot be washed out.

2 Randomly place seed stitches along the path within your guidelines.

3 Switch between different shades often.

4 The more you fill in the pathway, the fuller it will look. However, doing so is not necessary to achieve a nice effect.

RECOMMENDED SUPPLIES

Mottled gray 1mm-thick felt

Gray sewing thread

RECOMMENDED STITCH

Appliqué

Tack (Basting) Stitch (page 46)

INSTRUCTIONS

1 Cut out your boulder shape from the felt. Don't worry about being neat—most boulders aren't uniform in shape. Try to keep the bottom fairly flat, as that is where it meets with the earth or water.

2 Position the boulder in place on your canvas.

3 Make very small tack stitches around the edge of your boulder to secure it in place.

Water

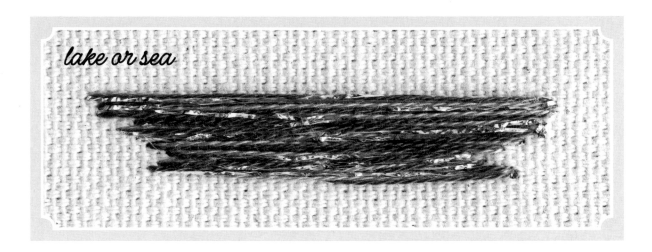

lake or sea

RECOMMENDED SUPPLIES

1 strand of dark blue-gray embroidery floss

1 strand of light blue-gray embroidery floss

Kreinik 001V Vintage Silver blending filament or silver sewing thread

RECOMMENDED STITCH

Stem stitch

INSTRUCTIONS

1 Combine all three strands of thread.

2 Horizontally make varying lengths of stem stitches across your lake or sea area.

3 Repeat haphazardly across the water area.

4 The more you fill in the area, the more water ripples and detail you will have, but it's absolutely not necessary for achieving a water effect.

TIP *Try changing the color of the water embroidery floss to brown and green to depict a still lake. The same effect can be used to create streams.*

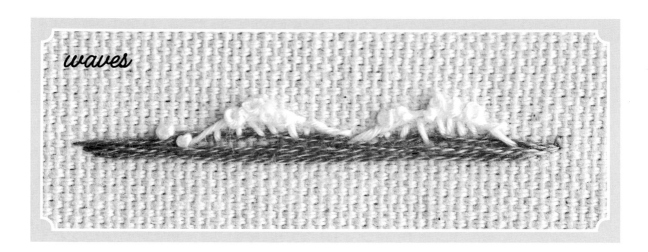

waves

RECOMMENDED SUPPLIES

2 strands of white embroidery floss

2 strands of light blue embroidery floss

2 strands of light blue-gray embroidery floss

RECOMMENDED STITCHES

Straight stitch

French knot

INSTRUCTIONS

1 Use the light blue-gray embroidery floss to makeshort sloping triangles with stem stitches where you want to place your waves. You don't need too many to achieve a nice effect—just two or three waves are all you need.

2 Make short vertical straight stitches to fill underneath your waves. While keeping them vertical, try not to be too neat, and even overlap a few here and there.

3 Top your waves with a choppy row of French knots. Vary the size of your French knots by changing the number of strands you use for each.

TIP 〰 *You can use the same method to create waves that are lapping the shore. In this case, add a few small French knots within the wave triangle.*

Trees and Shrubs

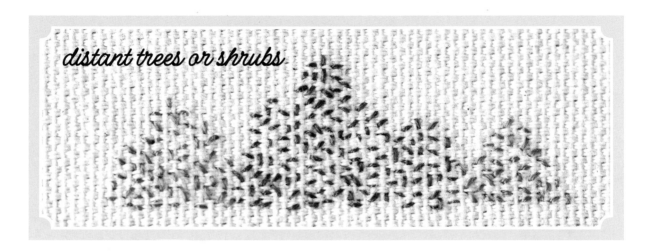

distant trees or shrubs

RECOMMENDED SUPPLIES

1–2 strands of dark green embroidery floss

RECOMMENDED STITCH

Seed stitch

INSTRUCTIONS

1 Create cloud shapes just above the horizon line of your canvas with very small seed stitches.

2 Make sure that the seed stitches are close together but not overlapping.

TIPS

• *Create the cloud shapes with one or two different shades of thread to depict different types of trees or shrubs in the distance.*

• *For a faster approach, try painting distant trees on your fabric. See Painted Clouds (page 53).*

pine tree

TIP ᕫ⌒ꕥ *Distant pine trees can be made from close and overlapping groups of vertical fern stitches along the horizon line.*

RECOMMENDED SUPPLIES

2 strands of dark brown embroidery floss

3 strands of dark green embroidery floss

RECOMMENDED STITCH

Straight stitch

INSTRUCTIONS

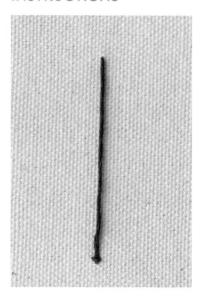

1 Make a long straight stitch the length of your tree trunk with the dark brown embroidery floss.

2. Stitch three short straight stitches ½″ (12mm) from the top of your trunk to join at the bottom with the dark green embroidery floss.

3. Stitch another group just below and to the right of the first three stitches.

4. Next, start making your tree spread out by stitching little groups of three on top of each other. Work diagonally toward the tree trunk.

5. Continue making diagonal branches down your trunk. Place an extra group of three every now and then in the center (or where you see a big gap).

6. Keep making wider branches until you reach the bottom of your tree. Then, add more groups of three where your tree looks a little bald.

RECOMMENDED SUPPLIES

Tree Trunk

1 strand of light brown embroidery floss

1 strand of medium brown embroidery floss

1 strand of dark brown embroidery floss

Tree Canopy

2–3 strands of medium green embroidery floss

RECOMMENDED STITCHES

Stem stitch

Detached chain stitch

INSTRUCTIONS

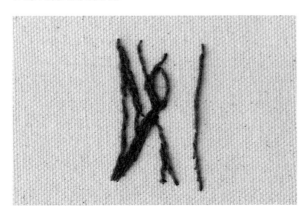

Start with the tree trunk.

1 Thread your needle with all three strands of brown embroidery floss.

2 Outline your tree. with stem stitches Then, makestem stitch haphazardly, snaking lines within your tree.

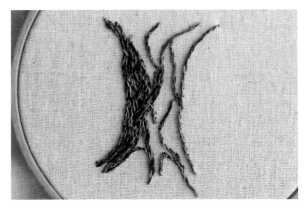

3 Continue making haphazard snaking lines inside your tree. Overlap the lines where you can for added dimension.

4 Stop when you have filled in the entire trunk of your tree. Fill in any tiny gaps you see in the bark with a dark color thread.

Tree Canopy

Next, fill in your tree canopy.

1 In branch-shaped groups, make detached chain stitches all over your tree canopy. Overlap the leaves for a bushier tree. Seed stitches can also be used to depict smaller leaves or canopies that are farther away.

2 Add a few stem-stitched twigs where you see gaps to depict hidden branches in the canopy.

TIP *Add a rougher texture to the bark with crewel wool thread (see Selecting for Texture and Effect, page 37). Or, skip the tree trunk altogether and add a draping canopy at the very top of your frame to depict a shady tree just out of view.*

palm tree

RECOMMENDED SUPPLIES

2 strands of medium brown embroidery floss

2 strands of medium green embroidery floss

RECOMMENDED STITCHES

Satin stitch

Fern stitch

INSTRUCTIONS

Start with the tree trunk.

1 Draw a slightly curved line on your canvas to represent your tree trunk. This line will act as your guide as you are stitching the trunk.

2 Starting at the tip of the trunk, make a very short row of satin stitches.

3 Move down a row along your guide line and make a slightly wider row of satin stitches.

Next, create the palm leaves.

1 At the tip of your trunk, draw a five- or six-pointed starfish shape. This shape will act as your guiding lines for your palm trees.

2 Starting at the tip of one of the lines, make fern stitches to form your palm leaf until you reach the trunk of the tree.

3 Repeat with your other palm leaves. It's okay if the leaves at the bottom of each palm overlap.

4 Continue in this fashion until you have reached the bottom of your trunk.

4 To create a bushier tree, fill in the gaps between your palm leaves with more palms.

cactus

RECOMMENDED SUPPLIES

3 strands of medium forest-green embroidery floss

Optional: beige embroidery floss

RECOMMENDED STITCHES

Chain stitch

INSTRUCTIONS

1 Start a continuous chain stitch at the top middle of your cactus and chainstitch down to its root.

2 Repeat with another continuous chain stitch on the left of your initial chain stitch.

3 Repeat with another continuous chain stitch on the right of your initial chain stitch.

4 Repeat in this fashion until the shape of your cactus is filled.

5 Optional: Make prickles all over your cactus with beige embroidery floss.

bushes or shrubs

RECOMMENDED SUPPLIES

2 strands of dark green embroidery floss

RECOMMENDED STITCH

French knot

INSTRUCTIONS

1 Start with a single French knot in the center of your bush.

2 Surround your first French knot with more French knots—no need to be neat.

3 Continue to add French knots until you reach the desired shape and size of the bush or shrub.

4 Optional: Add a short trunk at the bottom of your bush or shrub to depict a topiary bush.

TIP *Try creating a few French knots in other shades of green or use a variegated green floss to create more depth in your bush.*

Floral and Small Plants

grain

TIP ⌒ *Combine this shape with the Grassy Meadow (page 56) to create a wheat field.*

RECOMMENDED SUPPLIES

3 strands of medium yellow embroidery floss

1 strand of yellow-brown embroidery floss

RECOMMENDED STITCHES

Fern stitch

Straight stitch

INSTRUCTIONS

1 Start with the grain stalk. Make a tall vertical straight stitch with your yellow-brown embroidery floss.

2 About ½˝ (12mm) above the stalk, start your fern stitch and progress down toward the stalk tip.

3 Try to keep the wings of your fern stitch at the same width.

4 Finish the grain with a few small straight stitches poking out of your grain head.

RECOMMENDED SUPPLIES

1 strand of medium green embroidery floss

1 strand of lavender embroidery floss

RECOMMENDED STITCHES

French knot

Straight stitch

INSTRUCTIONS

1 Start with the lavender stalk. Make a tall vertical straight stitch with your green embroidery floss.

2 About ½″ (12mm) above the stalk, create a single French knot using the lavender embroidery floss.

3 Create two French knots just below your first French knot

4 Continue in this fashion until you reach the tip of the stalk.

TIP *There's no need to be too neat with your lavender. Haphazard flowers look more natural.*

RECOMMENDED SUPPLIES

2 strands of red embroidery floss

1 strand of light yellow embroidery floss

2 strands of medium green embroidery floss

RECOMMENDED STITCHES

Granitos stitch

Straight stitch

Detached chain stitch

INSTRUCTIONS

1 Create the tulip stalk with a long vertical straight stitch using medium green floss.

2 Combine the red and yellow embroidery floss.

3 Make a thick granitos stitch on top of the tulip stalk.

4 For the tulip leaves, using the green embroidery floss make a very long and thin detached chain stitch originating from the bottom of your tulip stalk.

TIP *Try choosing a variegated embroidery floss for your tulip flower and use it to create a field of tulips, all with slightly different colors and shades!*

RECOMMENDED SUPPLIES

DMC BLANC perle cotton #8 thread

2 strands of medium green embroidery floss

2 strands of light yellow embroidery floss

RECOMMENDED STITCHES

Straight stitch

French knot

Detached chain stitch

INSTRUCTIONS

1 Create the daisy stalk with a long vertical straight stitch using the medium green floss.

2 On top of the stalk, make a French knot using the light yellow floss.

3 Starting from the outside of the French knot, straightstitch short white petals with the perle thread. Only stitch a semicircle around the French knot.

4 For the daisy leaves, make a very long and thin detached chain stitch originating from the bottom of your daisy stalk with medium green floss.

RECOMMENDED SUPPLIES

1 strand of green-brown embroidery floss

2 strands of brown embroidery floss

1 strand of green embroidery floss

RECOMMENDED STITCHES

Straight stitch

Bullion knot

INSTRUCTIONS

1 With the green-brown embroidery floss, create a very long straight stitch slightly angled toward the left or the right.

2 Add a bullion knot with the brown emboridery floss on top of the stalk.

3 Make five or six straight stitches with the green embroidery floss, shorter than the reed stalk and angled toward the reed root. These will represent the leaves of the reed.

potted plant

TIP ✺ *You could replace the plant in this pot with any of the other small plants shown in this chapter, or use the techniques as inspiration to recreate your favorite plant!*

RECOMMENDED SUPPLIES

2 strands of green embroidery floss

2 strands of terra-cotta embroidery floss

RECOMMENDED STITCHES

Detached chain stitch

Satin stitch

Straight stitch

INSTRUCTIONS

1 Use your green embroidery floss to create a single vertical stitch the length of your plant stalk.

2 Along the stalk, add randomly placed detached chain stitches of the green thread. The more you add, the bushier your potted plant will become.

3 When you have finished adding your leaves, swap to the terra-cotta thread. Just below the bottom end of the plant stalk, create a row of vertical satin stitches. to form the base of your plant pot. Try to angle the stitches slightly outward toward the end.

4 On top of your pot base, create horizontal satin stitches, five or six stitches deep, until they just cover the top of the pot base and the bottom of the plant stalk.

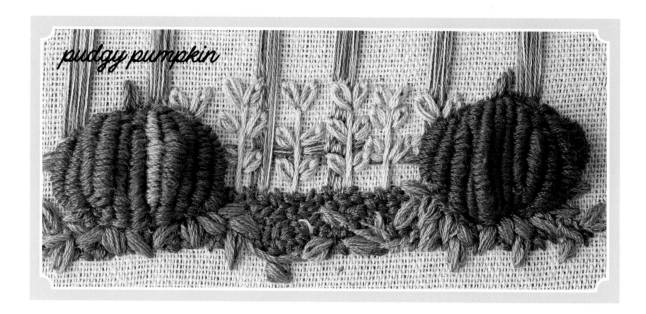

pudgy pumpkin

RECOMMENDED SUPPLIES

2 strands of light avocado-green embroidery floss

2 strands of copper terra-cotta embroidery floss

1 strand of sewing thread (color to match your felt)

1 square 2″ × 2″ (5 × 5cm) of dark green or terra-cotta felt

A pinch of polyester fiberfill or stuffing material of choice

RECOMMENDED STITCHES

Bullion knot

Straight stitch

Appliqué

INSTRUCTIONS

1 Cut a 1″–1½″ (2.5–4cm) pumpkin shape out of your felt. The shape can be irregular, but try to keep it mostly round or oval.

2 Place your felt pumpkin shape on the fabric where it will live.

3 Make tiny tack stitches around your felt shape with the sewing thread, leaving ³/₁₆″ (5mm) between each stitch. Leave ⅜″ (1cm) of space between the first and last tack stitch (see Tack [Basting] Stitch, page 46).

4 Gently stuff a small amount of fiberfill underneath your secured felt through the largest gap between your tack stitches. Add more stuffing as needed to make your pumpkin pudgier. (Do not overfill, as doing so will make the next steps more difficult.)

5 Close the stuffing hole with an additional tack stitch.

6 Thread your needle with terra-cotta embroidery floss. Starting in the center, at the bottom of your pumpkin shape, make a single bullion knot over your pumpkin shape, ending at the top center. This bullion knot will be your longest. It does not need to be neat; pumpkins have a lot of character, so yours will look great with a messy bullion knot or two.

7 Repeat this process on the left of your initial bullion knot. Get as close to your initial bullion knot as possible without overlapping.

8 Make a third bullion knot to the right of your initial bullion knot.

9 Repeat these steps until your felt pumpkin shape is covered. Each bullion knot will be progressively smaller as you work toward the edge of your felt shape.

10 Gently shape the bullion knots with the eye of your needle so they lay close to each other. Remember, it is okay to be a little messy.

11 Finish your pumpkin with two short straight stitches at the top center. Represent the pumpkin stalk with the avocado-green floss.

TIP ⌒⌢ *The end of a knitting needle or chopstick can help you stuff and shape your pumpkin.*

Brick, Stone, and Wood

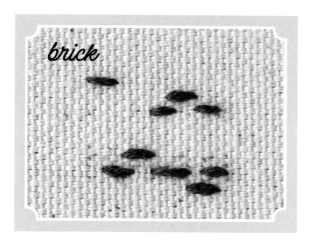

RECOMMENDED SUPPLIES

3–4 strands of brick-red embroidery floss

RECOMMENDED STITCH

Straight stitch

INSTRUCTIONS

1 Create scattered groups of short straight stitches to give the impression of bricks.

2 Make short straight stitches as randomly as possible, in groups of no more than five.

TIP ⌇ *For extra brick definition, scatter a single strand of beige thread in between your brick rows. Don't go overboard—just a few stitches will give you the impression you're looking for.*

- -

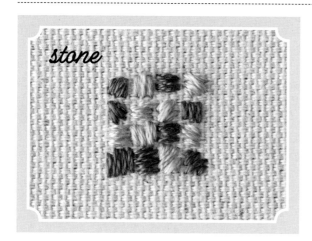

RECOMMENDED SUPPLIES

4–6 strands of light taupe embroidery floss

4–6 strands of medium taupe embroidery floss

4–6 strands of dark taupe embroidery floss

RECOMMENDED STITCH

Satin stitch

INSTRUCTIONS

1 Make a very short row of rough satin stitches in one of your taupe embroidery flosses.

2 Swap to a different color and satin stitch another very short row in an opposing direction to your first row.

3 Swap to your third color taupe and repeat the short row in an opposing direction to the first two.

4 Work the satin stitch diagonally as well as horizontally and vertically for a stone-wall effect.

5 Continue in this manner until you have filled the stone area on the canvas.

TIP ⌇ *Rather than short stones, you can also create longer neater stones for a cinderblock effect. Be sure to change your embroidery floss colors to more appropriate shades.*

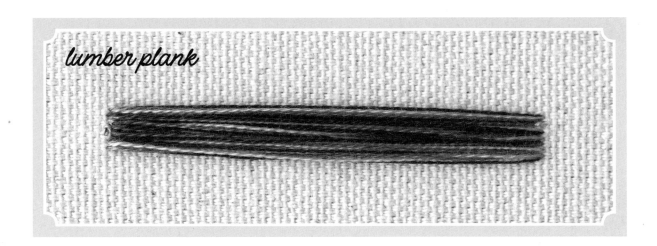

RECOMMENDED SUPPLIES

1 strand of light beige embroidery floss

1 strand of light brown embroidery floss

1 strand of dark brown embroidery floss

RECOMMENDED STITCH

Straight stitch

INSTRUCTIONS

1 Combine all three embroidery floss colors.

2 Make long straight stitches in the direction of the planks of your wall.

3 Stagger your straight stitches to convey a lumber wall. Don't focus on neatness—messy stitches look good here.

TIP *It takes a bit of time, but you can outline your straight stitches with a single strand of black or dark brown embroidery floss to better define your planks.*

how to get started

To get started, you'll need a piece of your chosen fabric that is at least 4″ (10cm) taller and wider than your chosen embroidery hoop or frame. For example, if you plan to stitch your piece in a 10″ (25cm) embroidery hoop, you will need a piece of fabric that is at least 14″ × 14″ (36 × 36cm).

Transferring Your Design

More than likely, you have a favorite way to transfer your designs onto your fabric. There is no one best way, so choose a method that makes you comfortable. Below, you'll find some methods I like to use, along with their pros and cons. Feel free to choose from these or use your own method.

running-stitch method

This is my favorite method to transfer a pattern onto fabric. It involves tracing the pattern onto tracing paper and placing the tracing paper on top of your fabric. Then, trace along the lines of your pattern with running stitches (page 43) of sewing thread. Once you have covered all your pattern lines, tear away the tracing paper to reveal your transferred pattern.

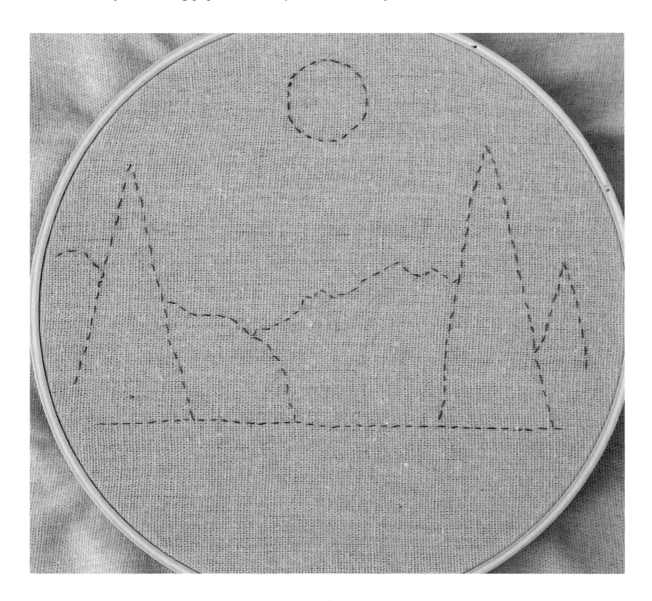

transfer pens

If I have little details or fine lines, this method is the one I use. Embroidery transfer pens are usually water- or heat-soluble, and each product comes with instructions. Note that some pens require you to trace your pattern, flip it, and then use heat to transfer the design onto your fabric. Using these pens means that you will end up with a mirror image of your design unless you reverse it prior to tracing. Follow the manufacturer's instructions for reversing your image if you do not want it to end up as a mirror image of your original sketch.

If you choose to use transfer pens, refer to the manufacturer's instructions for transferring your design and, later, removing any stray marks from your finished piece.

TIP ⟶ What to Transfer

The important thing to remember is that your embroidery will handle the detail. All you really need to transfer onto fabric are a few guiding lines to help you with size and placement. Write notes on your paper pattern or on your Design Development Worksheet to remind you of colors or concepts you want to capture.

want a little help?

At the end of this book are five Predesigned Projects (page 90) that you can use as practice projects or as bases for your own projects. Each of the five has a different theme and uses either the Pattern Library or a photograph to build the pattern.

Choose Where to Start

The hardest part of completing your embroidery project is making the first stitch. Once you get over that first hump, the rest will start to flow. It's helpful to remember that this project should be fun—nothing depends on it, and it's solely for your entertainment. Once you take the seriousness out of it, you'll find that building your happy place will make you a lot... happier!

think about layering

When choosing the exact object to start with, remember our lesson on Layering (page 35). To capture depth in your embroidered piece, you will want to layer your objects. This is easily achieved by thinking about the perspective of your happy place. What sits the farthest back? Start there!

Let's Start Together!

Now that you've chosen the place to start, let's get stitching!

1 Set up the fabric with your transferred design in your frame or hoop. Make sure that the fabric is drum-tight. If you are using a frame holder, get that set up, too, and then insert your embroidery frame.

2 Select the thread color, type, and (where applicable) the number of strands for your first object. Pull and snip off about a forearm's length of thread. Thread your needle.

3 Make a tiny stitch wherever you'd like to start your object. Secure it by overlapping the stitch once or twice.

4 Pick the first object to embroider and then refer to the technique instructions for that object in Stitching Your Elements (page 52).

5 Ready. Set. Stitch!

Continue on Your Own

Now that we've gotten over the first hump together, it's time for you to continue on your own! Here are some tips to help you on your journey.

don't sweat the small stuff

You may find that some techniques are just not looking right or are causing you frustration. It happens! The important thing to remember is that this project is meant to be fun. If you find yourself feeling irritated by a technique, it's not the end of the world to remove your stitches and start again or try something different. These situations give you the unique opportunity to dip into your own creativity by going beyond the book. Maybe you'll search for a different embroidery technique or adapt one of the other techniques in a different way. Remember, this is world is yours.

when you make a mistake

Every embroiderer in the world has messed up a stitch or two (or ten). There's nothing wrong with cutting stitches out and starting again. But before you grab the scissors, think about whether you can turn that so-called mistake to your advantage. Is it the mistake in a place that would welcome a messy stitch, such as a tree trunk? Can you stitch on top of it to give your piece more depth? Can you turn it into an additional detail in your design? Maybe it's not a mistake but a happy accident!

where to get help

I go to two places when I'm feeling stuck. First is the vast wealth of knowledge that is available for free on the internet. If I am struggling with a stitch, there are usually at least ten videos of that technique that I can study, to see where I am having trouble. Second, if I'm feeling uncreative, I turn to my mood board. What was it that I wanted to capture? What kind of feeling does it give me? That usually reignites my inspiration and gets me unstuck.

If all else fails, try taking a little break from your project. When you push through even though you are feeling irritated or uninspired, you'll learn to associate that activity with unpleasantness. Take a break and come back to it when you're feeling rested and excited to stitch.

How to Tell When You're Done

It can be tempting to keep embroidering object after object until your piece is filled to the brim with details. There's nothing wrong with this style if it reflects your happy place, but remember our lesson from choosing what to include in Putting It All Together: How to Design Your Happy Place (page 24). You only need a few core objects to convey your happy place. Once those core objects are done, think carefully about whether you need to add more.

If a space is calling to be filled, by all means, do so! However, if you're filling a space simply because this type of object **would** be there, consider leaving it out. For example, if your happy place is a vast wheatfield, do you really need all the hills and trees in the background, or should you focus on that one tree in the wheat field that you could sit under for hours?

If looking at your piece makes you smile, it's a sure sign it's complete.

finishing

Congratulations! You've completed your happy place! Now, it's time to add some finishing touches and get your happy place ready to display.

Finishing the Back

Chances are that the back of your piece looks pretty messy right now. That's a good thing! It means that you have worked really hard on your embroidery. To tidy your piece up, weave any long thread ends through the stitches on the back. Snip off any remaining pieces of thread that are dangling. Be careful not to clip too close to the fabric.

If you do not intend to wash your piece, you can secure the thread ends with fabric glue. Be careful not to use too much glue—just dab the stitch ends with a very small amount. Be sure to use a nonyellowing glue.

Washing Your Piece

I find that washing isn't always necessary, but it's a good idea if you used a dissolvable transfer method or if you can see any grime or dirt on the front of your piece. To wash your piece:

1 Run a shallow bath of tepid water in a clean basin. Add a few drops of a gentle fabric detergent. I like Woolite.

2 Very gently swish your piece in the water a couple of times to make sure that it is saturated.

3 Allow it to sit in the water for at least 20 minutes. Then, swish a couple more times to remove debris.

4 Repeat this process with clean water (no soap) to remove any remaining detergent.

5 Do not squeeze or wring your piece to remove water. Instead, lay it on a clean towel and roll the towel up with the embroidery piece inside. Leave for an hour and then remove.

6 Let it dry and then press out any creases with the gentle setting on your iron, avoiding your stitches. Alternatively you can place the embroidered piece facedown on a towel to avoid crushing your stitches.

Framing

Framing your piece often comes down to personal aesthetics. My favorite options are to frame my pieces either in the hoop or in a picture frame!

in the hoop

Many people like to frame their finished embroidery piece in the hoop they stitched it in. A hoop has the benefit of already being the perfect size, the tightening screw offers you ready-made hanging hardware, and backing the hoop is entirely optional. It's a very flexible option with a lovely cottage-core feel.

Some downsides are that it offers no protection for your work. It will gather dust, and the colors may change with exposure to the sun over time. You will also need to make sure that your fabric remains tight in the hoop, as the hardware may loosen over time, creating wrinkles in your finished piece.

To finish your piece in your hoop:

1 Examine your finished piece. If you see any dirt or grime, remove the piece from the hoop and wash it (see Washing Your Piece, page 85).

2 If you removed your piece for washing, place it back in the hoop. If you did not remove your piece, retighten the hardware as necessary.

3 Flip your piece over and, using a hand-sewing needle and sewing thread, make a running stitch to capture the excess edges of the fabric that are outside the hoop. Make long, loose stitches and pull to draw the edges of the fabric to the back of the hoop. Knot the thread when you have drawn all the excess fabric to the back.

4 Optional: If you wish to add a backing, cut a circle of wool felt just slightly smaller than the diameter of the hoop. Tack (Basting) stitch (page 46) the felt to the margins of the excess fabric to cover the back of the frame.

in a picture frame

Framing can give your final embroidery piece a really classy feel. A piece in a picture frame automatically looks more professional and is great for gifting!

Many premade embroidery frames allow you to simply slip in your finished piece, hoop and all. A quick online search for *embroidery frames* will get you a wide selection. You'll also find a number of stitching frames, so be sure that you select a frame intended for display.

If you opt to frame the piece yourself in a standard picture frame or shadow box, you need to follow just a few steps.

YOU WILL NEED

A square or rectangular frame in which to fit the finished embroidery area

A thin piece of foam core

Straight pins

Hand-sewing needle

Sewing thread

1 Examine your finished piece. If you see any dirt or grime, wash it (see Washing Your Piece, page 85).

2 Cut your piece of foam core ⅛" (3mm) smaller than the back opening of the frame.

3 Center your foam core over the back of your embroidery piece. Secure the embroidery along the edges of the foam core with straight pins.

4 Remove the glass from the frame and place the embroidery into the frame. Fold two of the parallel excess fabric edges over to the back of the piece.

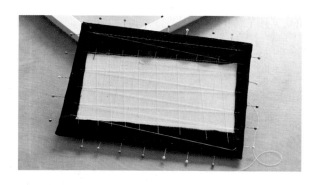

5 Thread your needle, make a knot, and stitch back and forth to lace the two pieces together to secure them. Knot the thread to end. Repeat with the remaining two edges.

6 Remove the straight pins, place the frame back on top, and secure.

professional framing

Your embroidery piece may not easily fit into a standard picture frame, especially if the stitches and fabric give it extra loft. For these reasons, you may choose to have your piece professionally framed, which can be expensive. However, if you love your work and you want it to last a lifetime, I recommend this method.

If you decide to professionally frame your piece, here are some rules to follow:

• Find a reputable framer—not just any framer but one who is experienced in handling textiles and, preferably, has worked with delicate pieces or embroidery.

• Ask for spacers. Your framer will probably do this automatically, but if you're not confident, ask them to put spacers in between the work (or mat) and the glass. This will keep the glass from touching your embroidery and squishing it.

• Ask for UV-protected glass. Regardless of where your piece will be hanging, this is a good idea. UV-protected glass will prevent UV rays from discoloring your embroidered happy place over time.

Congratulations!

Well done on bringing your happy place to life with embroidery! I hope that your embroidery makes you as happy as the place you depicted.

There is no limit to the number of pieces you can create. Why not make an entire world to fill your home or create one as a gift for someone else? These will act as a reminder of all the wonderful memories these places carry with them. Although you may not be able to visit your oasis in real life, through embroidery, it will always be near.

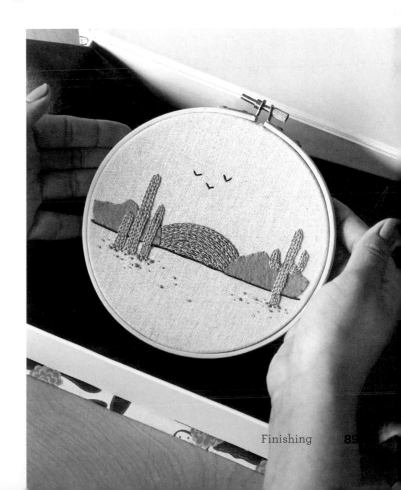

PREDESIGNED PROJECTS

The following projects can be created by using the techniques in this book. You can use them as practice projects, as jumping-off points, or as happy places all on their own. If you are using one of these as a jumping-off point, simply add, subtract, or substitute elements until you get the image from your inspiration.

Each project includes a template that you can transfer to your fabric and get started! If you don't want to photocopy the template from the book, you can download and print the project you wish to stitch. And, if you want to make one of the predesigned projects in a larger or smaller size, you can simply enlarge or reduce the template.

To access the templates through the tiny URL, type the web address provided below into your browser window. Print directly from the browser window or download the templates. ▶ **tinyurl.com/11559-patterns-download**

MY HAPPY PLACE

Fall Forest

Difficulty: Intermediate

MATERIALS

1 round 8″ (20cm) embroidery hoop

1 square 12″ × 12″ (30 × 30cm) muted green linen

Fabric paint in orange, red, yellow, and green

Optional: Fall Forest template

Tree Grove

2–3 strands of light drab brown, DMC 612 embroidery floss

2–3 strands of copper, DMC 921 embroidery floss

2–3 strands of red copper, DMC 919 embroidery floss

2–3 strands of dark golden brown, DMC 975 embroidery floss

2–3 strands of very dark mahogany, DMC 300 embroidery floss

Shrubs

1–2 strands of bright canary, DMC 973 embroidery floss

1–2 strands of very light yellow green, DMC 772 embroidery floss

1–2 strands of medium parrot green, DMC 906 embroidery floss

Grassy Meadow

1 strand of black avocado green, DMC 934 embroidery floss

1 strand of very light yellow green, DMC 772 embroidery floss

Oak Trees

2–3 strands of very dark mahogany, DMC 300 embroidery floss

2–3 strands of very dark straw, DMC 3852 embroidery floss

2–3 strands of bright canary, DMC 973 embroidery floss

Forest Floor and Pathway

6 strands of very dark beige brown, DMC 838 embroidery floss

6 strands of light cocoa, DMC 3861 embroidery floss

6 strands of very dark mahogany, DMC 300 embroidery floss

6 strands of medium old gold, DMC 729 embroidery floss

Hill at Horizon Line

1–3 strands of medium old gold, DMC 729 embroidery floss

1–3 strands of red copper, DMC 919 embroidery floss

techniques

Painted Clouds (page 53)

Grassy Meadow (page 56)

Earth or Fallen Leaves (page 59)

Oak or Maple Tree (page 65)

Tree Canopy (page 66)

Bushes or Shrubs (page 69)

Instructions

The template for this project is available for download. See the Pattern Library (page 114) for instructions on how to access the download that includes this template.

1 Transfer the design to your fabric with your favorite method (see Transferring Your Design, page 79).

2 Set up the fabric with your transferred design in your frame or hoop. Make sure that the fabric is drum-tight. If you are using a frame holder, get that set up, too, and then insert your embroidery frame.

3 Create a line of distant trees along the horizon line with the Painted Clouds technique. Use each of your fabric paint colors randomly. It's okay to overlap. Allow time to dry fully.

tree grove

1 With light drab brown, DMC 612 embroidery floss, make vertical straight stitches at varying heights to depict your tree grove tree trunks. Space them fairly close together, but not touching. Overlapping some is fine.

2 Use the Tree Canopy technique (page 66) and red copper, DMC 919 embroidery floss to create patches of tree-grove canopy above the tree trunks. Try to fill in your canopy as much as possible, but a few gaps here and there are fine.

3 Using the same technique, but with very dark mahogany, DMC 300 embroidery floss, fill out your tree-grove canopy a little more. This time, work the stitches underneath your original patches to create a shadowy effect, depicting leaves deeper in the canopy.

4 Using the same technique, follow with copper, DMC 921 embroidery floss and then dark golden brown, DMC 975 embroidery floss.

shrubs

Beneath the tree grove, add small shrubs in bright canary, DMC 973 embroidery floss; very light yellow green, DMC 772 embroidery floss; and medium parrot green, DMC 906 embroidery floss.

grassy meadow

1 Using the Grassy Meadow technique, fill in the top layer of your grassy meadow with very light yellow green, DMC 772 embroidery floss.

2 Using shorter straight stitches, fill in the bottom layer of the grassy field with black avocado green, DMC 934 embroidery floss. Rather than filling in a thick layer, make this layer a little patchier.

oak trees

1 Starting with the back oak tree, use the Oak or Maple Tree technique to fill in the trunk with very dark mahogany, DMC 300 embroidery floss.

2 Before starting on the canopy, fill in the front oak tree's trunk with the same technique and thread.

3 Fill in the back tree canopy with seed stitches of very dark straw, DMC 3852 embroidery floss. Try to keep your stitches small and close together. Top the canopy on the left with bright canary, DMC 973 embroidery floss to depict leaves bathed in sunshine.

4 Fill in the canopy of the front tree with the same technique. Make your stitches slightly larger than in the back canopy. This is your opportunity to add more leaf detail by forming your stitches into an oak-leaf shape. Use very dark straw, DMC 3852 embroidery floss and bright canary, DMC 973 embroidery floss in patches to depict light bouncing off sections of the canopy.

forest floor and pathway

1 Using the Earth or Fallen Leaves technique, begin with the pathway that curves around your oak trees. Use different colors and sprinkle the seed stitches until you have filled the pathway area.

2 After the pathway has been filled, move on to the hillside beneath the tree grove. Make smaller stitches at the back of this area (remove a strand of thread for a distance effect).

3 Finish your piece with random patches of grass in very light yellow green, DMC 772 embroidery floss.

finishing

Use your favorite method to finish the back of your hoop (see Finishing, page 84).

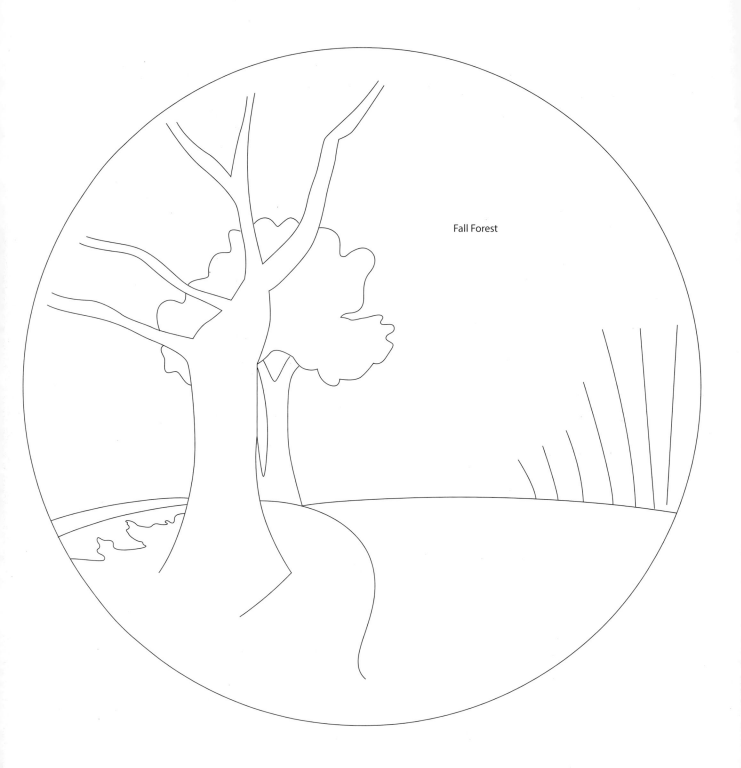

Fall Forest

Seaside

Difficulty: Intermediate to Advanced

MATERIALS

1 round 8″ (20cm) embroidery hoop

1 square 12″ × 12″ (30 × 30cm) sky-blue linen

Optional: Seaside template

Palm Trunk

2 strands of medium mocha brown, DMC 3032 embroidery floss

Palm Leaves

1 strand of very dark parrot green, DMC 904 embroidery floss

1 strand of light avocado green, DMC 470 embroidery floss

Beach

1 strand of very light old gold, DMC 677 embroidery floss

1 strand of light mocha brown, DMC 3782 embroidery floss

1 strand of light drab brown, DMC 612 embroidery floss

Sea

1 strand of medium baby blue, DMC 334 embroidery floss

1 strand of medium very dark blue, DMC 312 embroidery floss

Kreinik Silver 001HL blending filament or silver sewing thread

Waves

1 strand of baby blue, DMC 3756 embroidery floss

Reeds

1 strand of taupe sewing thread

Sea Grass

1 strand of light avocado green, DMC 470 embroidery floss

1 strand of topaz, DMC 725 embroidery floss

1 strand of very dark parrot green, DMC 904 embroidery floss

Birds

1 strand of black, DMC 310 embroidery floss

techniques

Instructions

The template for this project is available for download. See the Pattern Library (page 114) for instructions on how to access the download that includes this template.

1 Transfer the design to your fabric with your favorite method (see Transferring Your Design, page 79).

2 Set up the fabric with your transferred design in your frame or hoop. Make sure that the fabric is drum tight. If you are using a frame holder, get that set up, too, and then insert your embroidery frame.

palm trees

1 Start your stitching with the trunk of your palm tree, using medium mocha brown, DMC 3032 embroidery floss.

2 Next, move on to the palm leaves. You will use one thread color for each leaf. Choose the first of your green thread colors and complete the first palm leaf. Start from the length you would like your palm head to be away from your trunk and move toward the center, finishing at the tip of your tree trunk.

3 Follow with more palm leaves in a circular pattern. Resist the urge to space the leaves evenly. Think about how a bushy palm tree behaves in the wild. The leaves at the tip are probably jutting out, while the leaves at the bottom are probably heavy, as they are laden with all the leaves above them. Try to mimic that look with your stitching.

4 Repeat the process with your second green color, filling in some of the gaps you left your first time around your palm tree head.

5 Make a final pass around your palm tree head again with your first color. By this point, your palm tree head should be filling out nicely.

6 When you have finished the third layer, look at your palm tree head and consider whether it looks full enough. If not, add more leaves. Consider the fact that these leaves are on the outside of the tree, so you may want to use a lighter shade of green to depict sun glancing off the leaves.

7 When your first tree is complete, move on to the second.

beach sand

1 Combine all three strands of your beach color.

2 Fill in your beach area, working from bottom to top. Try to lay your threads close together, but not overlapping.

sea

1 Combine all three strands of your sea color.

2 Starting from the top of your beach line and working upward to the horizon line, fill in your sea area. Try to lay your threads close together, but not overlapping.

3 Finish with two or three waves that lap over the first couple of rows of your beach sand. Plunge your needle through some strands of your beach to secure the waves and avoid gaps caused by your needle.

beach banks

1 Start with your beach reeds, using your taupe sewing thread. Place your reeds at different heights and varying distances from each other.

2 Once you have added as many beach reeds as you like, move on to the sea grass, using one thread color for each blade. Moving from dark colors to light, slowly fill in the beach bank area, covering the bottom of your palm tree trunk entirely, moving from dark to light colors as you progress.

3 Once your beach bank is filled, finish it with a row of short grass along the bottom.

birds

Create a small flock of birds midflight in your blue sky. Vary the height and width of each of your fly stitches to depict birds in different stages of movement.

finishing

Finish the back of your hoop with your favorite method (see Finishing, page 84).

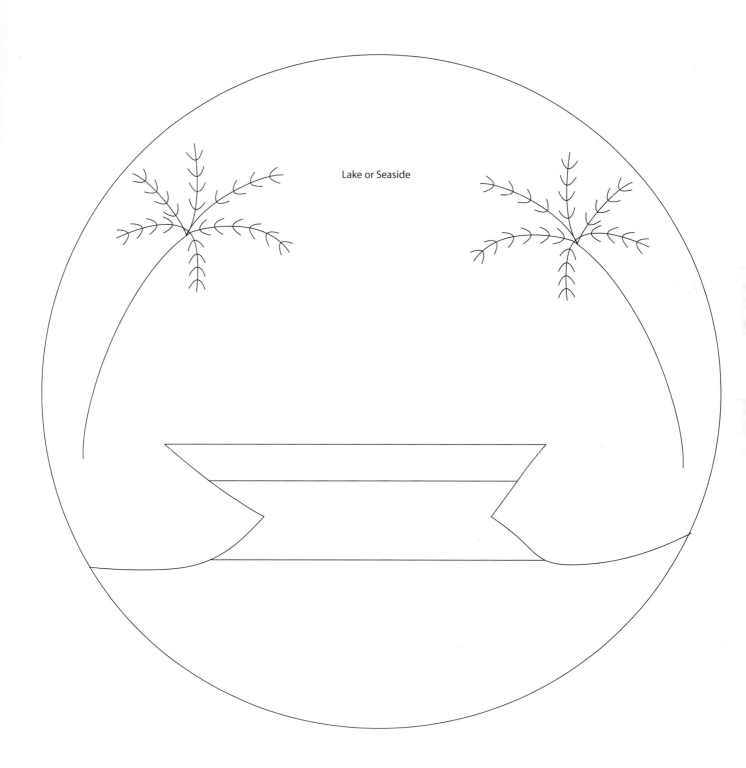

Lake or Seaside

Mountaintop Meadow

Difficulty: Intermediate

MATERIALS

1 round 8" (20cm) embroidery hoop

1 square 12" × 12" (30 × 30cm) black or navy blue linen

Optional: Mountaintop Meadow template

Moon and Stars

1 strand of metallic silver sewing thread

Clouds

White and black or dark gray fabric paint

Pine Trees

2 strands of dark pine green, DMC 3362 embroidery floss

2 strands of dark fern green, DMC 520 embroidery floss

Mountains

1 strand of medium tin, DMC 03 embroidery floss

1 strand of dark tin, DMC 04 embroidery floss

Mountain Meadow

1 strand of very light drab brown, DMC 613 embroidery floss

1 strand of medium green gray, DMC 3052 embroidery floss

1 strand of medium pistachio green, DMC 320 embroidery floss

1–3 strands of dark lavender, DMC 209 embroidery floss

1–3 strands of dark lemon, DMC 444 embroidery floss

techniques

Painted Clouds (page 53)

Sun and Moon (page 54)

Stars (page 55)

Grassy Meadow (page 56)

Distant Trees or Shrubs (page 63)

Pine Tree (page 64)

Lavender (page 71)

Daisy (page 72)

Instructions

The template for this project is available for download. See the Pattern Library (page 114) for instructions on how to access the download that includes this template.

1 Transfer the design to your fabric with your favorite method (see Transferring Your Design, page 79).

2 Set up the fabric with your transferred design in your frame or hoop. Make sure that the fabric is drum-tight. If you are using a frame holder, get that set up, too, and then insert your embroidery frame.

moon

Start your project by stitching your moon.

clouds

1 Place two or three cloud formations below your moon. As this is a nighttime scene, mix some of the black or gray fabric paint with the white to paint the bottom of your cloud.

2 Top the cloud with white fabric paint.

pine trees

Starting from the top and working down, fill in your pine trees. You have two pine tree colors; use the dark to fill in the side farthest from the moon and the lighter color to fill in the side closest to the moon and at the tip. This technique will give you a shadow effect.

mountains

1 To depict pine trees in the distance, fill in your mountain shapes with very short vertical straight stitches.

2 Use the darkest of your mountain colors to fill in both mountain sections from bottom to top.

3 Line the top of your mountain, closest to the moon, with the lightest of your mountain colors to depict light shining on the trees at the top of your mountain.

mountain meadow

1 Use one strand of dark lavender, DMC 209 embroidery floss to create tiny lupins underneath your mountain range. You are trying to capture distance, so keep your flowers small and scattered.

2 Use one strand of the dark lemon, DMC 444 embroidery floss to create two very small straight stitches that meet in the middle. They will depict mountain daisies in the distance, so keep your flowers small and scattered. Leave blank space in between your flowers to depict a dark meadow with a few hints of flowers that catch the light of the moon.

3 In the foreground, create a close-up of the flora in your mountain meadow. Start with the mountain flowers, using the Daisy and the Lavender techniques and two or three strands of yellow and lavender thread.

4 Follow your flowers with your grass, using the Grassy Meadow technique. Use one strand of green color per grass blade.

Finish your piece by adding scattered stars made with the metallic silver thread.

Finish the back of the hoop with your favorite method (see Finishing, page 84).

Mountaintop Meadow

Desert

Difficulty: Beginner

MATERIALS

1 round 6" (15cm) embroidery hoop

1 square 10" × 10" (25 × 25cm) oatmeal linen

Optional: Desert template

Sun

2 strands of gold sewing thread

Mountains

1 square 6" × 6" (15 × 15cm) square 2mm-thick deep coral felt

1 strand of coral sewing thread

2 strands of ultra very dark topaz, DMC 780 embroidery floss

Cactus

3 strands of medium pistachio green, DMC 320 embroidery floss

Pebbles

2 strands of very light beaver gray, DMC 3072 embroidery floss

2 strands of medium tin, DMC 03 embroidery floss

Birds

1 strand of black, DMC 310 embroidery floss

techniques

Sun and Moon (page 54)

Birds (page 55)

Appliqué Hill (page 57)

River Pebbles (page 59)

Cactus (page 69)

Instructions

The template for this project is available for download. See the Pattern Library (page 114) for instructions on how to access the download that includes this template.

1 Transfer the design to your fabric with your favorite method (see Transferring Your Design, page 79).

2 Set up the fabric with your transferred design in the frame or hoop. Make sure that the fabric is drum-tight. If you are using a frame holder, get that set up, too, and then insert the embroidery frame.

sun

Create your setting sun with the Sun and Moon technique, but rather than create a full circle, you will create a semicircle. It is the same technique, except you will start and stop along your horizon line. To save on thread, when you end one line, start the next line just to the side of where you ended.

mountains

1 Cut out the mountain shapes from your felt. You can use the pattern as a guide for the shapes.

2 On either side of the sun, appliqué the felt mountains to your canvas with the coral sewing thread.

3 From left to right, stem stitch one long line with two strands of ultra very dark topaz, DMC 780 embroidery floss.

cactus

Create your cactus shapes.

pebbles

1 Combine all four strands of your pebble colors.

2 Randomly place pebbles beneath the cacti. Be sure to cover the base of each of the cacti. Vary the thickness and width of the pebbles for a more natural look.

birds

Create a small flock of birds midflight in your sky. Vary the height and width of each of your fly stitches to depict birds in different stages of movement.

finishing

Finish the back of the hoop with your favorite method (see Finishing, page 84).

Desert

Left Mountain

Right Mountain

Pumpkin Patch

Difficulty: Intermediate to Advanced

MATERIALS

1 pair 8″ (20cm) stretcher bars

1 pair 10″ (25cm) stretcher bars

1 rectangle 12″ × 14″ (30 × 36cm) oatmeal linen

Optional: Pumpkin Patch template

Earth

3 strands of dark mocha beige, DMC 3862 embroidery floss

Fence

1 strand of very light drab brown, DMC 613 embroidery floss

1 strand of khaki brown, DMC 167 embroidery floss

1 strand of light drab brown, DMC 612 embroidery floss

Bean Shoots

3 strands of light yellow green, DMC 3348 embroidery floss

Pumpkins

2 squares 3″ × 3″ (8 × 8cm) orange felt

1 strand of orange sewing thread

3 strands of medium parrot green, DMC 906 embroidery floss

3 strands of golden brown, DMC 3826 embroidery floss

Fall Leaves

2 strands of medium tangerine, DMC 741 embroidery floss

1 strand of lemon, DMC 307 embroidery floss

techniques

Pudgy Pumpkin (page 74)

Lumber Plank (page 77)

Potted Plant (page 73)

Oak or Maple Tree (page 65)

Earth or Fallen Leaves (page 59)

Instructions

The template for this project is available for download. See the Pattern Library (page 114) for instructions on how to access the download that includes this template.

1 Transfer the design to your fabric with your favorite method (see Transferring Your Design, page 79).

2 Set up the fabric with your transferred design in the frame or hoop. Make sure that the fabric is drum-tight. If you are using a frame holder, get that set up, too, and then insert the embroidery frame.

3 Position and attach the felt for the pumpkins. You won't be filling them yet, but you will want them in position so you can embroider around them first.

earth

Fill in the earth portion of the pumpkin patch.

fence

1 Combine all of your thread colors.

2 Create the fence with the Lumber Plank technique.

bean shoots

Using the plant portion of the Potted Plant technique, create five or six bean shoots over the fence, being careful not to disturb the fence stitches too much.

pumpkins

1 Complete the pumpkins with the Pudgy Pumpkins technique. Use medium parrot green, DMC 906 embroidery floss on one or two of the bullion-knot rows to depict a not-quite-ripe pumpkin.

2 Underneath the pumpkins, use medium parrot green, DMC 906 embroidery floss and the tree canopy technique to create a bushy seat for the pumpkins. You can cover each of the detached chain stitches with one straight stitch so that the leaves look fuller.

fall leaves

1 Combine all of your fall leaf colors.

2 Use the tree canopy technique to create overhanging branches from an out-of-sight oak tree.

3 Add a few leaves mid-drop and on the earth of the pumpkin patch to add the illusion of motion to your piece.

finishing

Finish or frame the piece with your favorite method (see Finishing, page 84).

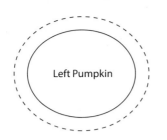

Left Pumpkin

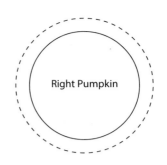

Right Pumpkin

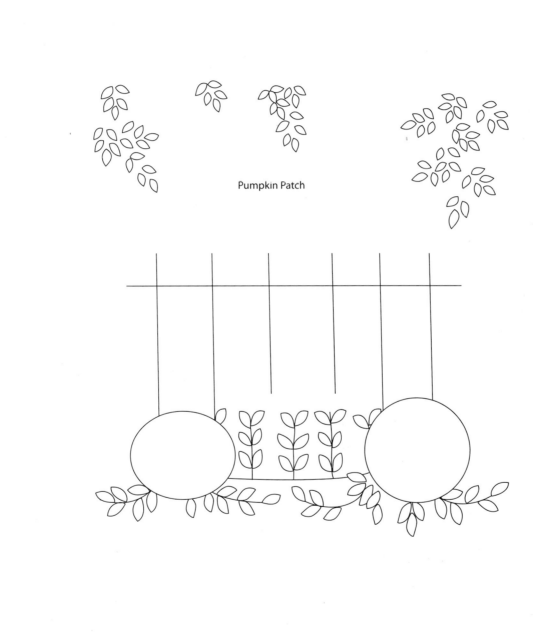

Pumpkin Patch

pattern library

In this chapter, you'll find an exclusive library of print-ready patterns designed to help you easily create and design your happy place! You can use the library items to build your happy place piece by piece, or you can mix and match individual elements with your own patterns. The objects in the library are designed to fit with each other, within a 10″ (25cm) embroidery piece. If you are creating a 10″ (25cm) piece, you can print out the motifs you require as is, but keep in mind that not every object in your embroidery design will be the same scale. For a smaller embroidery piece or to portray distance, you will need to reduce some objects to fit the required scale. For larger embroidery pieces or for closer objects, you may need to enlarge some motifs. Don't be afraid to enlarge and reduce a few times to get just the right effect.

If none of the objects included pique your interest, don't be afraid to draw them as you imagine them or trace a shape from a photograph. Remember, you don't need to be an artist—you just need a simple outline and then the stitches do the heavy lifting!

Accessing the Motifs

To make life a little easier for you, all the motifs in the image library can be downloaded in two different formats. To download a PDF containing the full-size image library, type the web address provided below into your browser window. You can then download the PDF containing the full library and print the pages you wish to use. ▸ **tinyurl.com/11559-patterns-download**

If you wish to use any of the library motifs in a larger, smaller, or altered format, we've provided a download file containing all the images in the library. To access the images through the tiny URL, type the web address provided below into your browser window. You can then download the image files. ▸ **tinyurl.com/11559-patterns-download**

Making the Most of the Library

You can use the motifs as is or reduce or enlarge them, but that isn't all you can do! You can change up what you use the motif to create, and you can flip, elongate, widen, and rotate the motifs.

In step 3 of Instructions for Building Your Design (page 31), you can see that I chose to use the Meandering Path motif as a stream instead of as a path.

If the motif you want is facing in the wrong direction for your design, you can place the image into a word-processing document and flip it so that it faces the other direction. Refer to the instructions for the document program you are using to find out how to flip images.

If you want your motif to appear taller, you can stretch the image vertically. Be aware that when you stretch the image vertically, it will become narrower, so this won't work for all the motifs! In the example below, the mountain becomes more dramatic as it becomes taller.

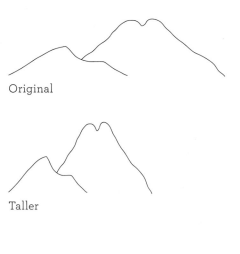

Original

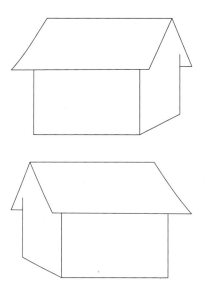

Taller

Images can also be widened to create a different effect. As with stretching an image, widening will appear to flatten the image, making it shorter. This can distort the motif, so this technique won't work for all of them. By widening the Meandering Path motif, you can create a roadway or even a lazy river.

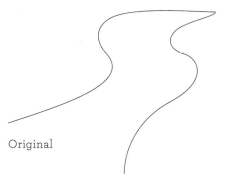

Original

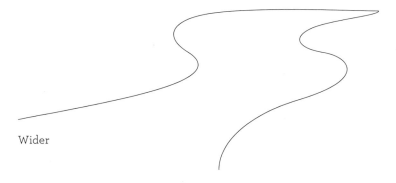

Wider

If your composition is looking a bit too perfect, consider placing one or more of the motifs at an angle. Don't be afraid to play. Manipulate them and apply various techniques to get a wider variety of effects. Use your imagination and, most importantly, have fun!

Library Motifs

PINES

OAK/MAPLE

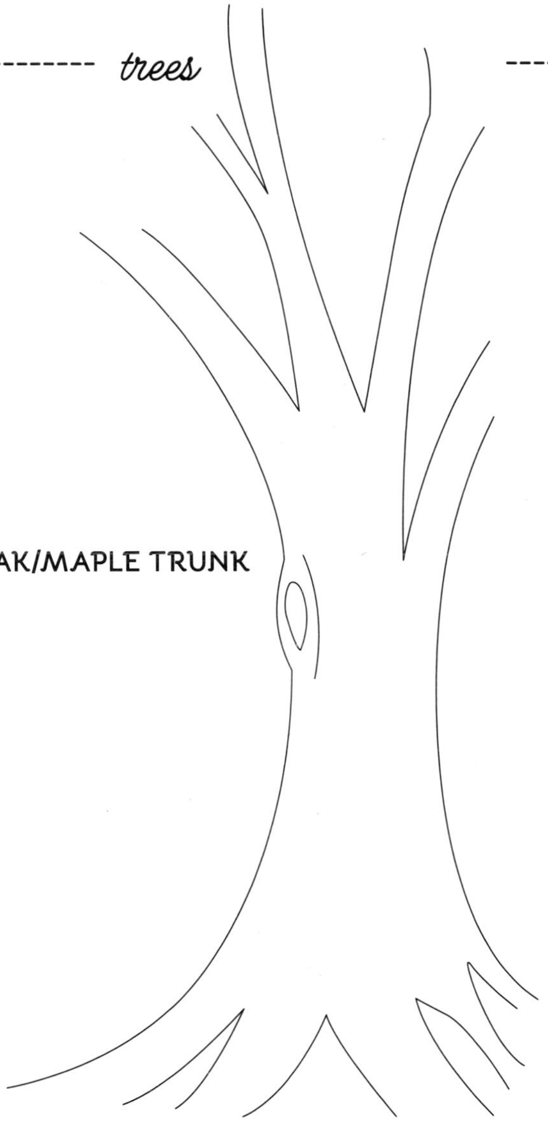

OAK/MAPLE TRUNK

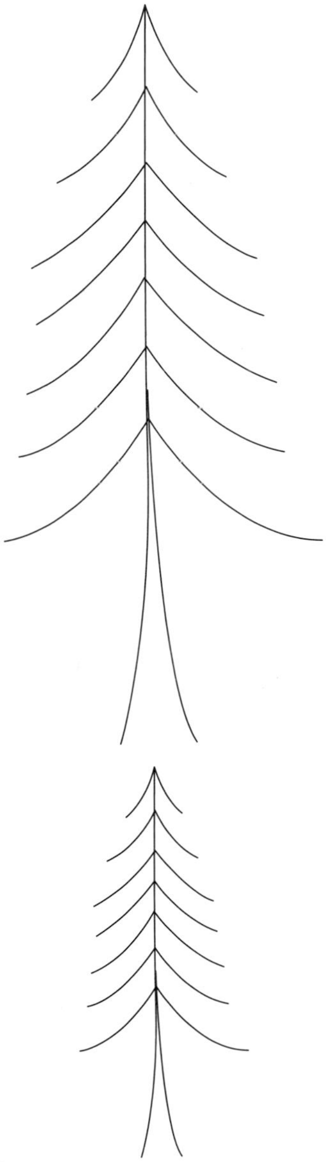

PALM

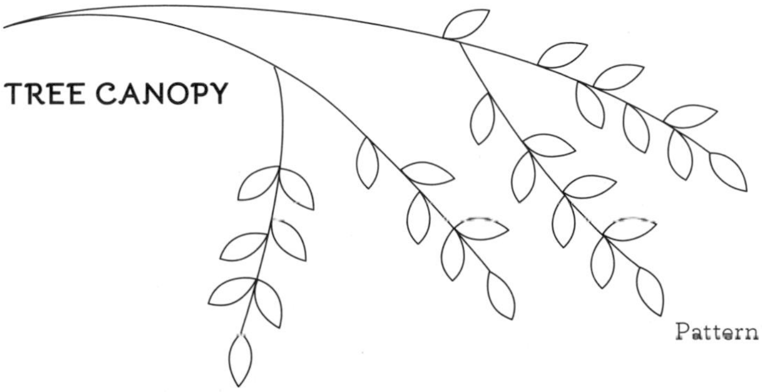

TREE CANOPY

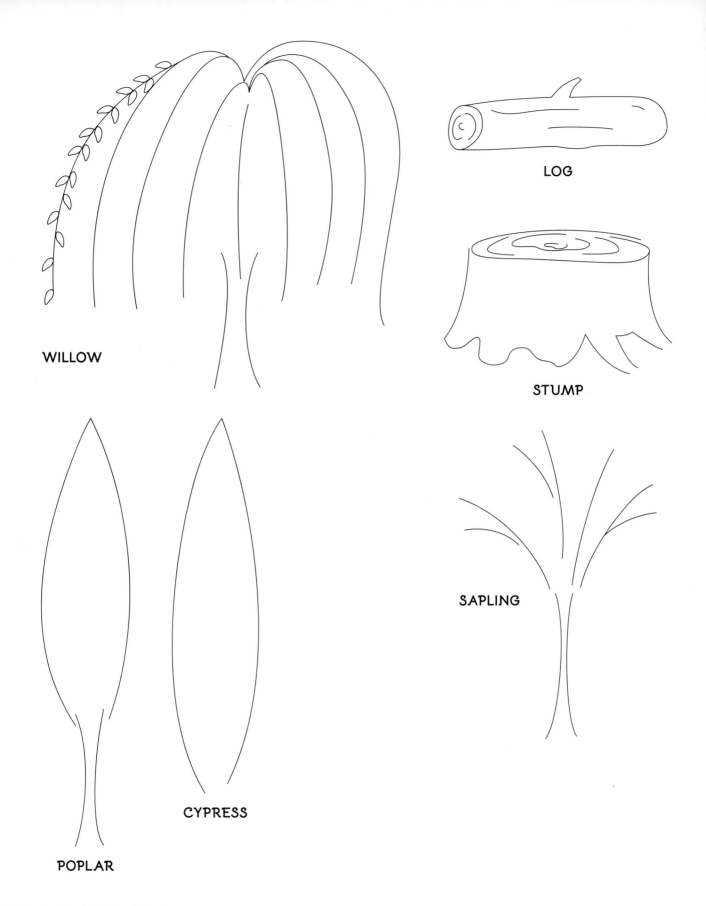

WILLOW

LOG

STUMP

SAPLING

POPLAR

CYPRESS

plants and bushes

BUSHES

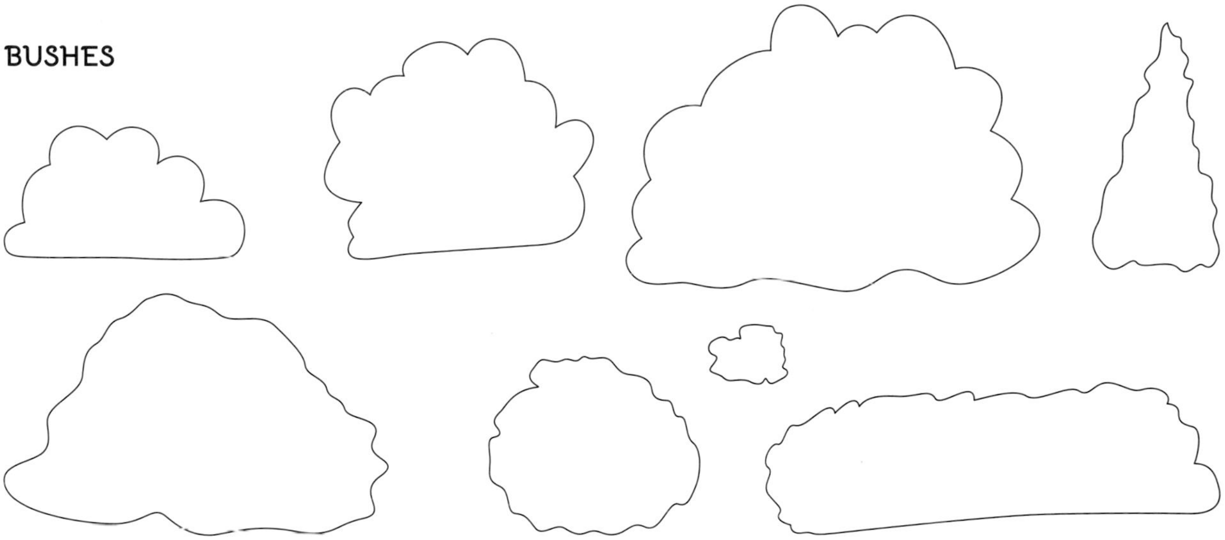

FERN

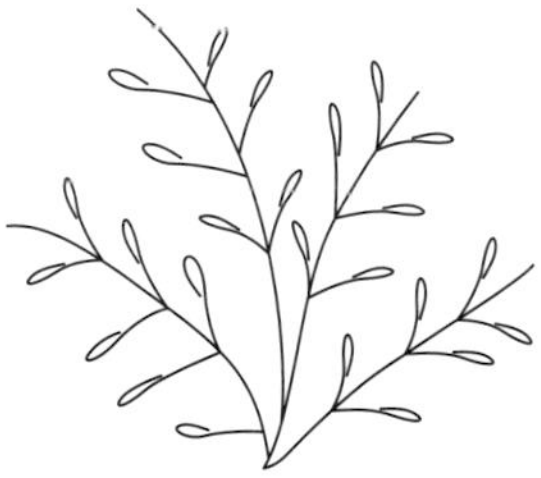

POTTED PLANT

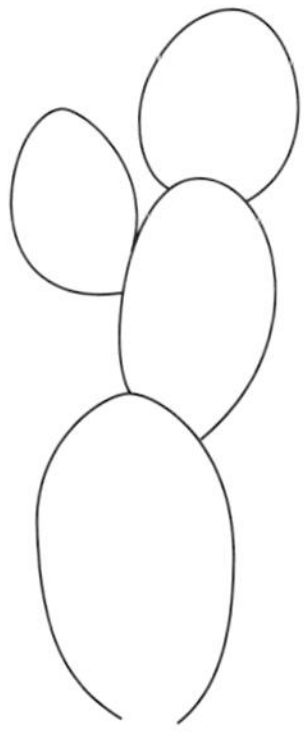

TULIP

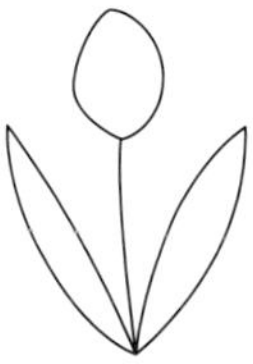

LAVENDER

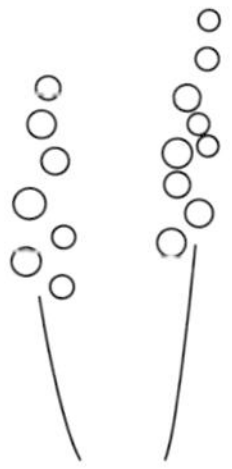

VINE

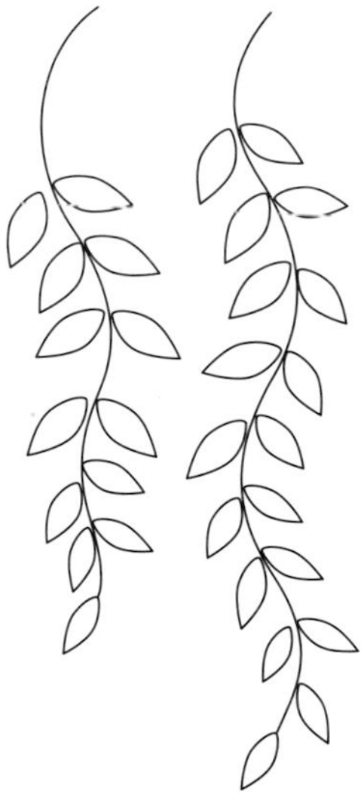

CACTI

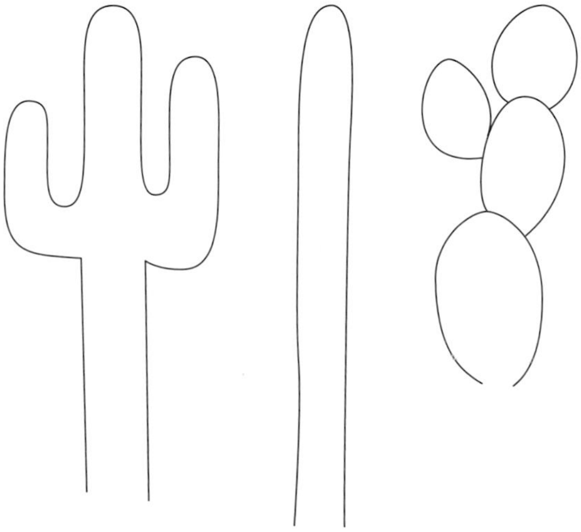

TUMBLEWEED

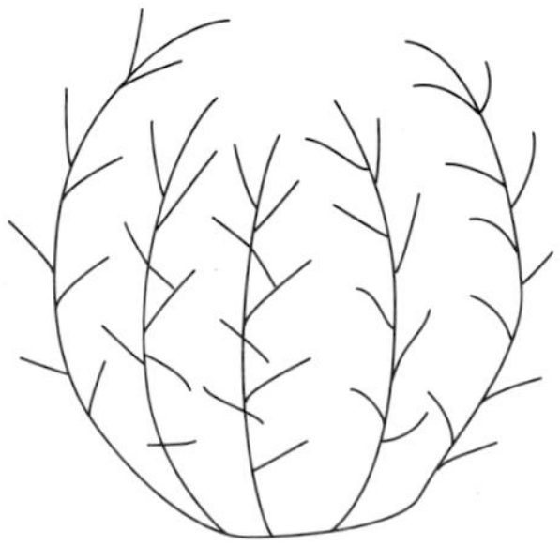

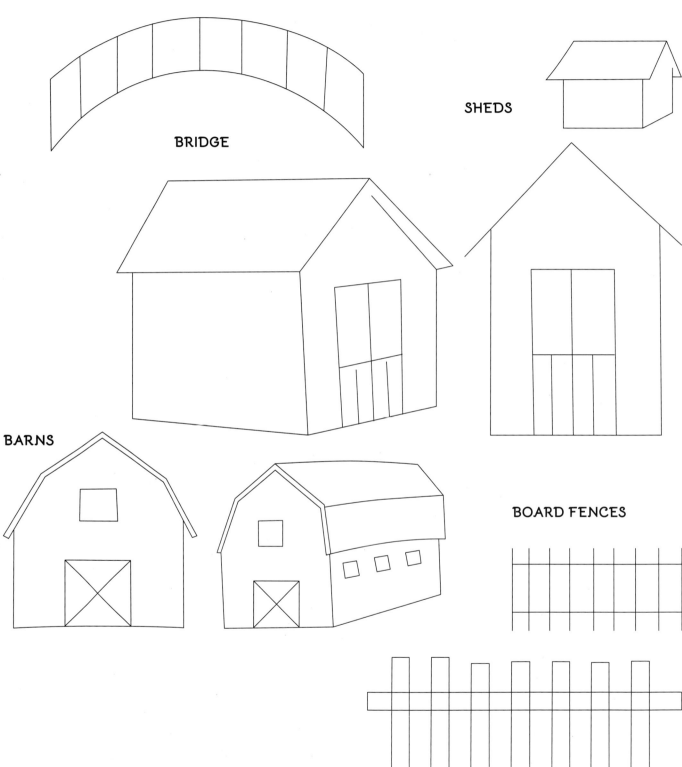

BRIDGE

SHEDS

BARNS

BOARD FENCES

RAIL FENCE AND GATE

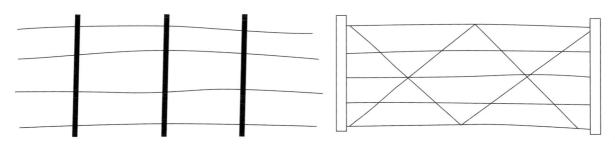

STONE FENCE

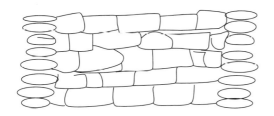

PICKET FENCE

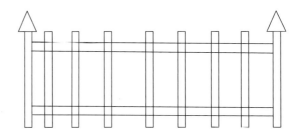

TRELLIS

GAZEBO

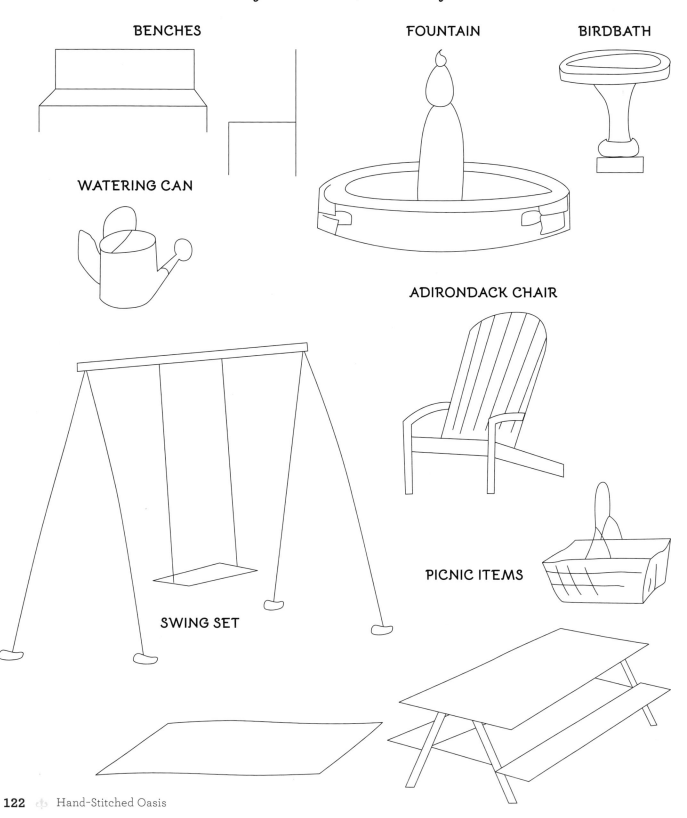

BENCHES

FOUNTAIN

BIRDBATH

WATERING CAN

ADIRONDACK CHAIR

PICNIC ITEMS

SWING SET

CAMPER

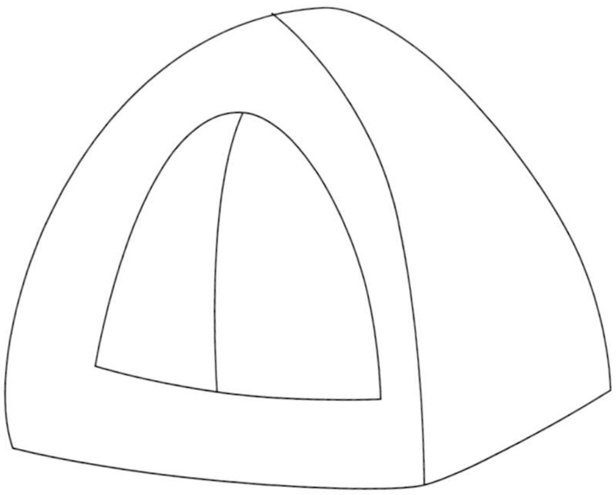

TENTS

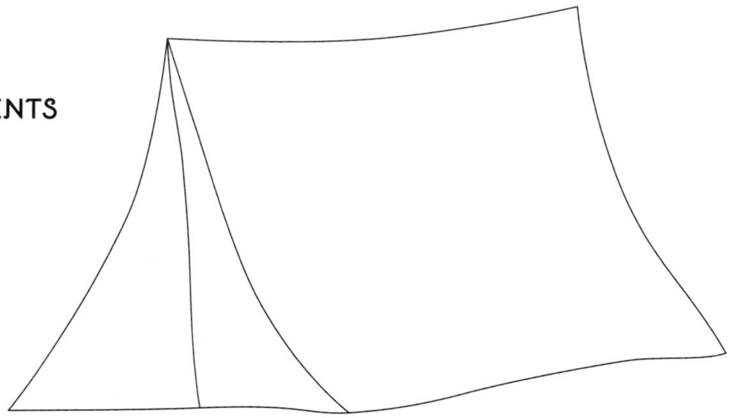

CAMPFIRE

CAMP CHAIR

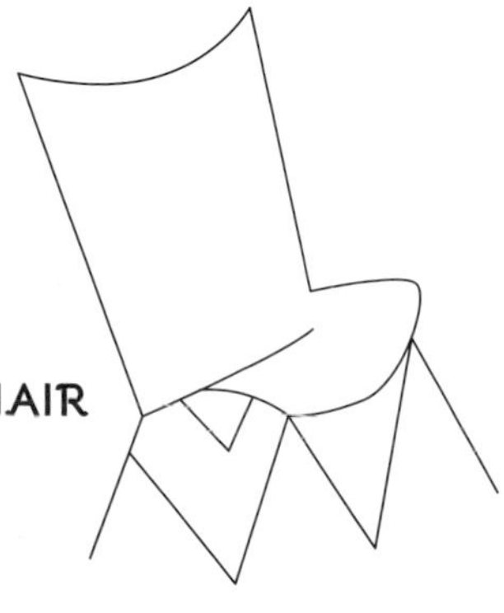

DOCK

SAILBOAT

BOAT

LIGHTHOUSE

CANOES

BEACH CHAIR

ROWBOATS

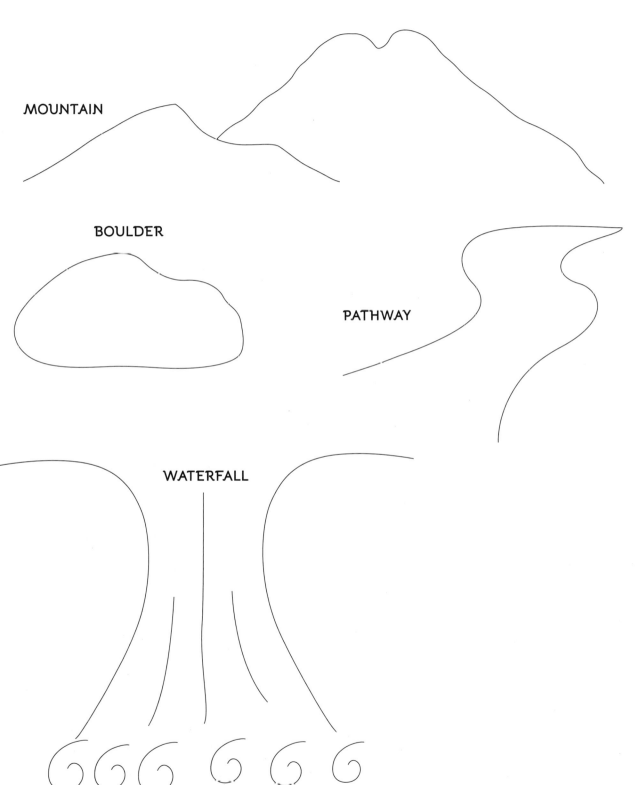

MOUNTAIN

BOULDER

PATHWAY

WATERFALL

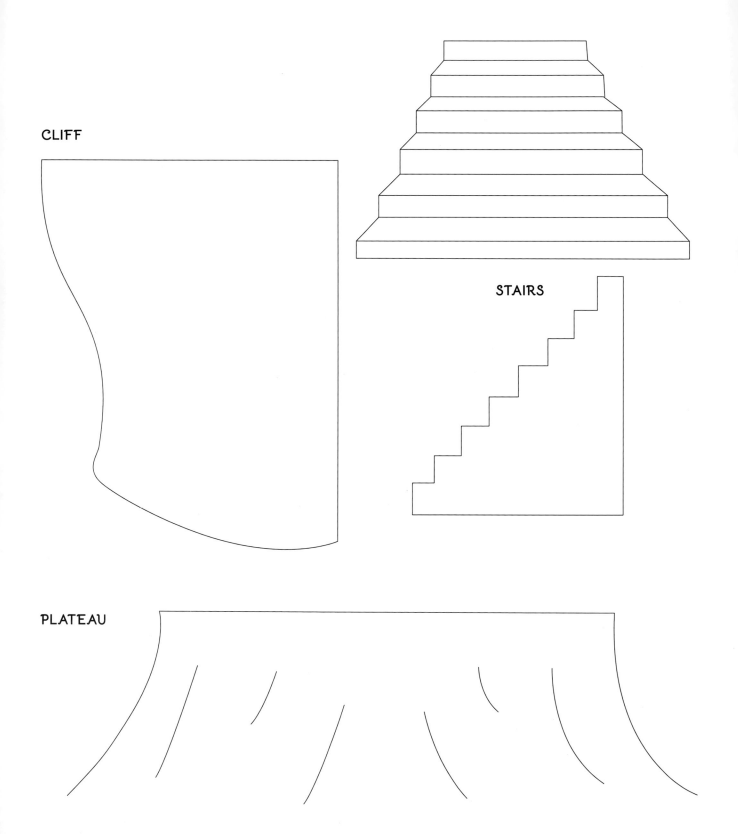

CLIFF

STAIRS

PLATEAU

ABOUT THE AUTHOR

Loving all things fiber has been a life-long pursuit of Theresa Lawson. After years of dabbling in a variety of fiber crafts, Theresa discovered and fell in love with how embroidery can be used to create masterpieces from seemingly innocuous materials.

Raised in the English town of Bury St Edmunds, Theresa moved across the world to Seattle in the United States. Here, she created a portfolio of work and soon became known for her detailed and whimsical embroidered pieces. Fans of her work were particularly taken with her embroidered houses.

Now working from her studio on Lummi Island, Theresa creates embroidered art and patterns, surrounded by the inspiration of mountains, forests, and wildlife.

See more of Theresa's work at themonsterslounge.com.

CREATIVE SPARK

ONLINE LEARNING

Embroidery courses to become an expert embroiderer...

From their studio to yours, Creative Spark instructors are teaching you how to create and become a master of your craft. So not only do you get a look inside their creative space, you also get to be a part of engaging courses that would typically be a one or multi-day workshop from the comfort of your home.

Creative Spark is not your one-size-fits-all online learning experience. We welcome you to be who you are, share, create, and belong.

Scan for a gift from us!

For a list of other fine books from C&T Publishing,
visit our website to view our catalog online.

C&T PUBLISHING, INC.

P.O. Box 1456 | Email: ctinfo@ctpub.com
Lafayette, CA 94549 | Website: ctpub.com

Tips and Techniques can be found at
ctpub.com/quilting-sewing-tips.

For quilting supplies:

COTTON PATCH

1025 Brown Ave.
Lafayette, CA 94549
Store: 925-284-1177 | Email: CottonPa@aol.com
Mail order: 925-283-7883 | Website: quiltusa.com

Note: Fabrics shown may not be currently available, as fabric
manufacturers keep most fabrics in print for only a short time.

CRAFTS/Needlework/Embroidery

CAPTURE YOUR HAPPY PLACE
❋ with embroidered vignettes ❋

STITCH various textures, from foliage and water to pavement and pathways, to personalize your landscape composition

EMBROIDER five starter projects and add personalized outdoor details to reflect your happy place

LEARN 35 techniques to create realistic details and get step-by-step instructions for basic stitches

stash BOOKS®

ctpub.com

11559   US $26.95 / GBP 16.9
ISBN-13: 978-1-64403-412-
52695

9 781644 034125

T2-EUX-608

Also available as an eBook